Uncle Dan's Report Card

Books by Barbara C. Unell

GETTING YOUR CHILD FROM NO TO YES:
WITHOUT NAGGING, BRIBING, OR THREATENING
Jerry L. Wyckoff, PhD, and Barbara C. Unell

DISCIPLINE WITHOUT SHOUTING OR SPANKING:
PRACTICAL SOLUTIONS TO THE MOST COMMON
PRESCHOOL BEHAVIOR PROBLEMS
Jerry L. Wyckoff, PhD, and Barbara C. Unell

HOW TO DISCIPLINE YOUR SIX TO TWELVE YEAR OLD
WITHOUT LOSING YOUR MIND
Jerry L. Wyckoff, PhD, and Barbara C. Unell

THE EIGHT SEASONS OF PARENTHOOD:
HOW THE STAGES OF PARENTING CONSTANTLY RESHAPE
OUR ADULT IDENTITIES
Barbara C. Unell and Jerry L. Wyckoff, PhD

20 TEACHABLE VIRTUES:
PRACTICAL WAYS TO PASS ON LESSONS OF VIRTUE
Barbara C. Unell and Jerry L. Wyckoff, PhD

Uncle Dan's Report Card

From Toddlers to Teenagers,
Helping Our Children
Build Strength of Character
with Healthy Habits
and Values Every Day

BARBARA C. UNELL AND BOB UNELL

A PERIGEE BOOK

A PERIGEE BOOK
Published by the Penguin Group
Penguin Group (USA) Inc.
375 Hudson Street, New York, New York 10014, USA

Penguin Group (Canada), 90 Eglinton Avenue East, Suite 700, Toronto, Ontario M4P 2Y3, Canada
(a division of Pearson Penguin Canada Inc.)
Penguin Books Ltd., 80 Strand, London WC2R 0RL, England
Penguin Group Ireland, 25 St. Stephen's Green, Dublin 2, Ireland (a division of Penguin Books Ltd.)
Penguin Group (Australia), 250 Camberwell Road, Camberwell, Victoria 3124, Australia
(a division of Pearson Australia Group Pty. Ltd.)
Penguin Books India Pvt. Ltd., 11 Community Centre, Panchsheel Park, New Delhi—110 017, India
Penguin Group (NZ), 67 Apollo Drive, Rosedale, Auckland 0632, New Zealand
(a division of Pearson New Zealand Ltd.)
Penguin Books (South Africa) (Pty.) Ltd., 24 Sturdee Avenue, Rosebank, Johannesburg 2196,
South Africa

Penguin Books Ltd., Registered Offices: 80 Strand, London WC2R 0RL, England

While the authors have made every effort to provide accurate telephone numbers and Internet addresses at the time of publication, neither the publisher nor the authors assume any responsibility for errors or for changes that occur after publication. Further, the publisher does not have any control over and does not assume any responsibility for author or third-party websites or their content.

First edition: August 2011

Library of Congress Cataloging-in-Publication Data

Unell, Barbara C., 1951–
    Uncle Dan's report card : from toddlers to teenagers, helping our children build strength of character with healthy habits and values every day / Barbara C. Unell and Bob Unell.—1st ed.
        p.   cm.
    Includes index.
    ISBN 978-0-399-53677-9
    1. Child rearing.   2. Parent and child.   3. Moral development.   4. Children—Conduct of life.
5. Virtues—Study and teaching.   I. Unell, Bob.   II. Title.
    HQ769.U4754   2011
    649'.7—dc22   2011013728

PRINTED IN THE UNITED STATES OF AMERICA

10 9 8 7 6 5 4 3 2 1

Most Perigee books are available at special quantity discounts for bulk purchases for sales promotions, premiums, fund-raising, or educational use. Special books, or book excerpts, can also be created to fit specific needs. For details, write: Special Markets, Penguin Group (USA) Inc., 375 Hudson Street, New York, New York 10014.

In loving tribute to
DANIEL LEON BRENNER
1904–2002
Our Uncle Dan

And all of the "Uncle Dans" of the past, present, and future

CONTENTS

Contents

FOREWORD

When Barbara and Bob Unell first approached me with Uncle Dan's Report Card, I was thrilled—what a great opportunity to bring together parents, students, teachers, and communities, while connecting the past with the present.

Schools do an excellent job of developing our children's intellect. But we must also develop their character. This challenge requires the efforts of teachers and schools, to be sure, but also of families and communities.

Aristotle suggested that just as one becomes a lyre player by practicing the lyre, we become virtuous by practicing virtue. Uncle Dan's Report Card asks children, as well as their parents and teachers, to reflect upon those parts of daily life that signify a person of strong character: kindness, reliability, consideration of others, integrity, and honesty.

Foreword

Reinforcing the good habits of strong character will help our children excel in and out of the classroom, as well as throughout their lives as members of families and communities. As our children grow older, they will face new and difficult ethical choices. Uncle Dan's Report Card can help our children understand our shared values and how those values inform choices in everyday life.

We have an awesome responsibility to succeeding generations. Together, we can advance the intellectual and character development of all children.

KATHLEEN SEBELIUS
Governor of Kansas
May 2, 2005

The Discovery of Uncle Dan's Report Card

We can only be said to be alive in those moments when our hearts are conscious of our treasures.

—THORNTON WILDER

My Grandmother's Dining Room Table
OCTOBER 1959

My grandmother's dining room table was the center of celebration. All of our special occasions were celebrated there. The dishes, the silverware, everything was perfectly in place. Cloth table cover, cloth napkins folded just right. So many colorful foods. Never just one entrée. And I always seemed to disappoint my grandmother when I did not eat seconds and even thirds. But the helpings were so big in the first place!

Tonight, I had already finished but stayed at the table. Uncle Dan always made a speech. And the children couldn't go play until he did.

We were all in awe of Uncle Dan. Even the adults held him

in the highest regard. As the oldest sibling on my mother's side, Dan wore the title of "big brother" well. He took care of everyone in the family. Whether it was for legal advice, career moves, or business tips, Dan was the man you would turn to for guidance.

But as I grew up, Uncle Dan gave me something more precious than advice. He gave me the inspiration to follow my dreams, eagerly making time to listen to me, as if I were the most important person in the whole world. I had no idea that he was a revered leader in the community and the country. I just knew that he believed in me, and his unconditional love mattered more to me than words and reason. And he made me feel as if my life mattered just as much to him.

Indeed, people from all walks of life were attracted to Dan. He was always so dapper, no matter the occasion or day of the week, so striking in his three-piece suits, sparkling silver cuff links and crisp, white monogrammed dress shirts. He had never been married, but we were all his "children." He seemed to be more than an uncle. We had other uncles in the family, but he was the family sage.

He never sought out the limelight, but corporations, nonprofit organizations, and universities sought him out to serve on their boards of directors for his wisdom and moral character. His focus always on the greater good, Dan found success as a judge, a partner in the law firm that carried his name, and president of the University of Missouri Board of Curators, his proudest accomplishment. To our family, however, he was the man who we all loved, who always had a seat reserved for him in the big chair at the head of the dining room table.

Now everyone was crowded into the dining room around that chair. It was dead silent. Uncle Dan cleared his throat and took a drink of water. He tapped his mouth with his handkerchief, and then he started to talk.

"I want to say how nice it is that we are all here together. I want to thank Grandma Tillie for this wonderful dinner. You children should know how important it is to have such a wonderful family. Your mothers and fathers work hard to help you and care for you. They want to make sure that you have the opportunity to go to school, to go to college. That's why it's so important for you to work hard, get good grades, and make your parents proud."

It always started like that. The message was always about family, community, and education.

Uncle Dan had so much to teach us. Not all of it was taught to us in his after-dinner speeches. Sometimes we would go to big dinners in fancy places where a lot of people would honor Uncle Dan. He was always volunteering his time to help different charities. And as I got older, people would tell me how Uncle Dan had helped them in a very big way by paying for school or assisting in their adoption of a baby.

But tonight was one of the extra-special family dinners because my cousins and I all had just received our report cards. We knew that if we had done well, Uncle Dan would give us money. A lot of money. Like twenty dollars!

President Harry S. Truman and Daniel Leon Brenner.

We all knew that *the question* was coming. He cleared his throat and asked, "Well, how are your grades?"

I was excited to tell Uncle Dan about my grades because I had done well this term. And then I realized I had never asked Uncle Dan about his grades. I got up enough courage to ask.

"Pretty well . . . I did pretty well. My favorite subject was history. I got an E in history."

What's an E? We all wanted to know.

"An E stood for 'Excellent,' G for 'Good,' M for 'Medium,' and P for 'Poor.'"

We were sure that Uncle Dan had received nothing but E's on his report card, but we never asked him. He was the smartest person we had ever known.

My Dining Room Table
FAST-FORWARD 43 YEARS

As always, the table got quiet. Now it was in my house. My dining room, with my children included around the table. Yet it was still my grandmother's table, refinished to its original condition. It was time for Uncle Dan's after-dinner speech.

The evening was late for him. He was so weak. His eyes were barely opened. It took all of his energy to do it. He cleared his throat and began to talk. "I want to thank Bunny and Bob." Maybe a little slower. Maybe a little weaker. Yet the message was still the same . . . the importance of family, community, and education.

Around the table he went, asking us about our community or school work.

Our children were now in college. How many times over their lives did they answer these questions? Yet they seemed as excited as ever to report to their great-uncle. Our son had put together the "Good Sport Award" for his college television station. Our daughter was producing a concert to raise money for charity. My husband shared how he was volunteering to help teach marketing at our inner-city arts academy. And just as if I were still ten years old, I couldn't wait to give my report. Now, instead of my grades, it was about my work to teach children virtues in our public school district.

As we all proudly reported our community accomplishments, Uncle Dan listened intently and continued to nod his head slowly up and down in approval. "Wowzee," he exclaimed, his ultimate expression of delight.

Little did I know that this would be the last family dinner with Uncle Dan. The last time he would give his speech. It was my birthday, just six weeks before his death.

The Discovery
OCTOBER 2002

Just two days before his ninety-eighth birthday, Uncle Dan passed away in my arms. He had lived a long, happy, and healthy life. It was only five years earlier that he had retired from his law practice.

A few weeks had passed, and I was ready to take care of his estate. I had mixed emotions—still grieving, yet knowing that he would want me to buckle down and do the task ahead of me with care and intelligence.

I was in his bedroom sorting through his belongings. His closet. His cashmere coat. His fedora. His ties. Stains from important dinners dotted the dress shirts waiting to be laundered. His wall of plaques, awards, and photographs. Photos with Presidents Truman, Johnson, Nixon, and Ford.

I noticed a set of dusty bookends holding lots of papers on top of his dresser. A small, yellow, folded card caught my eye. As I opened it, my heart started to pound. The cover read: "Kansas City, Kansas, Public Schools. School and Home Report Card."

The front cover of Uncle Dan's 1914 report card.

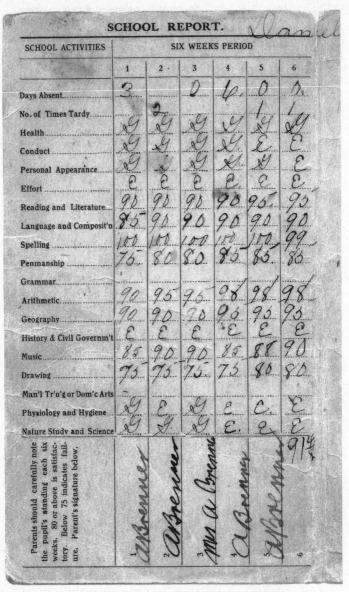

SCHOOL REPORT. *Daniel*

SCHOOL ACTIVITIES	SIX WEEKS PERIOD					
	1	2 ·	3	4	5	6
Days Absent	3		2	6	0	0
No. of Times Tardy		2			1	1
Health	G	G	G	G	G	G
Conduct	G	G	G	G	E	E
Personal Appearance	G		G	G	G	E
Effort	E	E	E	E	E	E
Reading and Literature	90	90	90	90	95	95
Language and Composit'n	85	90	90	90	90	90
Spelling	100	100	100	100	100	99
Penmanship	75	80	80	85	85	85
Grammar						
Arithmetic	90	95	95	98	98	98
Geography	90	90	90	96	95	95
History & Civil Governm't	E	E	E	E	E	E
Music	85	90	90	85	88	90
Drawing	75	75	75	75	80	80
Man'l Tr'n'g or Dom'c Arts						
Physiology and Hygiene	G	E	G	E	E	E
Nature Study and Science	G	G	G	E	E	E

Parents should carefully note the pupil's standing each six weeks. 80 or above is satisfactory. Below 75 indicates failure. Parent's signature below,

1. Brenner
2. A Brenner
3. Mrs A Brenner
4. A Brenner
5. A Brenner
6. 91¾

On the left side of Uncle Dan's report card was the "School Report."

HOME REPORT.

HOME ACTIVITIES	SIX WEEKS PERIOD					
	1	2	3	4	5	6
Books Read	15	12	13	10	15	
Letters Written	0	1	0	1	3	
Hours Worked	0	0	0	0	0	
Money Earned	100	200	300	100	100	
Money Saved	100	175	250	75	75	
Things Made	0	0	0	0	0	
Evenings at Home	42	42	42	42	42	
Care of Teeth	G	G	G	G	G	
Regular Bathing	G	G	G	G	G	
Care of Clothing	G	G	G	G	G	
Sleeping, Windows Open	Go	G	E	m	G	
Manners	M.	M	G	M	M	
Helping Father	G	G	G	G	G	
Helping Mother	G	G	G	G	G	
Morning Duties	G	G	G	G	G	
Evening Duties	G	G	G	G	G	
Obedience & Promptness	E	E	E	G	G	
Habits of Kindness	G	G	G	G	G	
Truthfulness and Honesty	E	E		E	E	
Mark the first seven with the number; the remainder with "E" for Excellent, "G" for Good, "M" for Medium, "P" for Poor. Parent's signature below.	A Brener	a Brener	Mrs a Brener	a Brener	a Brener	

On the right side of Uncle Dan's report card was the "Home Report."

All pupils in the grade schools, whose average for the last six weeks period of the term is 80 or above with a grade in any study not below 75, shall be promoted without question. An Average between 75 and 80 with a grade in any study not below 60 shall be carefully considered by Supervising Principal and teacher. A pupil shall not be promoted whose general average in the four basic studies of his grade is not 75 or above. The grade in the last column is the standing of the child. No average is made. The last record is the grade.

The worth of the child cannot be measured in terms of "Per cent" alone. The home life of the child is an important part of the whole life. The teacher's judgment will be a much better one if the home will kindly co-operate. Parents are asked to carefully consider and mark "Home Report" as indicated.

M. E. PEARSON, Superintendent.

On the back cover of Uncle Dan's report card was a message from the superintendent.

The blanks were filled in with marks from a fountain pen.

Pupil: Daniel Brenner
Enrolled 9-14 191<u>4</u> in 5th grade

Promoted 5-28 191<u>5</u> to 6th grade
John Ingalls School
Lois Huggins Teacher
Rose McIlwain Principal

On the back cover was a message from the Superintendent:

The worth of the child cannot be measured in terms of "Per cent" alone. The home life of the child is an important part of the whole life. The teacher's judgment will be a much better one if the home will kindly cooperate. Parents are asked to carefully consider and mark "Home Report" as indicated.

Signed
M. E. PEARSON, Superintendent

I opened the card to see two sides.

On the left side, it read: SCHOOL REPORT. On the right side, it read: HOME REPORT.

I now knew what he was doing all of those years in his after-dinner speeches: Uncle Dan was giving us our own Home Reports!

It was as if I had uncovered the Dead Sea Scrolls of my family. I couldn't wait to share this treasure that Uncle Dan had kept on his dresser for nearly ninety years. My husband said it was a miracle that I, with my professional background in parenting and moral education, was the one who had made this discovery. Anyone else, he said, would have thrown the little yellow report card away.

I showed it to teachers. I showed it to my friends. Everyone asked the same questions: What happened to this? Can we bring this back? How?

Anyone who was close to education or parenting knew the challenges. Parental involvement in school was challenging . . . Educators were grappling with how to keep their classrooms safe. Parents were juggling work and home, family and friends. Children were in day care and soccer; and in the hustle and bustle, the lessons of Uncle Dan's report card were fading from our society like the ink of my grandmother's fountain pen.

Calling Kathleen
MARCH 2005

One early spring day, I awoke with the idea to meet with my U.S. congressman, Dennis Moore. He had always been a great supporter of my husband and my projects. Congressman

Moore's eyes welled up with tears when I told him about the program. He began to talk about his father. Then he excused himself and left the room to return with a small box that he said belonged to his wife. Inside was a beautiful badge signifying reaching the goal of "perfect attendance" throughout all of elementary school. Fifty years later, she knew right where it was!

"I don't think we can make Uncle Dan's report card into law," the congressman said, "but I know someone who I think will be very interested in helping us." He arranged a meeting with the governor, Kathleen Sebelius.

During our meeting the governor began to outline a plan that she referred to as a pilot program for school and home, called Uncle Dan's Report Card, to test its impact on children's behavior today. She selected three school districts across the state to represent different populations: Dodge City, a rural district; Blue Valley, a suburban district; and Kansas City, an urban district.

We created a modern version of the Home Report, complete with a fun character, named Uncle Dan, of course! The goals were to motivate and encourage children to happily follow and mark their own Uncle Dan's Report Card each day, and inspire parents to share their children's Uncle Dan's Report Card with their teacher. By doing so, parents and teachers would come together to help children build good behavior habits that would lead to success in school and in life. As we went to each district and each school one by one, the educators were surprised. They wondered: Where is the kit? The thick binders? The DVDs for instruction and training? We explained there were no fancy training materials. Just the report card.

Who Is Your Uncle Dan?
APACHE ELEMENTARY, 2007

"Where do you put your important papers that you take home from school?" Uncle Dan (aka my husband) asked the children at the assembly.

"In my backpack."

"In my folder!"

"I keep my important papers in my briefcase," said Uncle Dan. "And I have a very important paper I brought to school today to share with you! Here it is! Uncle Dan's Report Card!" He proudly pointed to the large cartoon character whose image was revealed on the poster, as he unfolded it. "Look, it's me!" My husband was dressed just like the character: blue pants, white shirt, red tie, and even black glasses. His hair wasn't nearly as full as my uncle's beautiful white shock; but as far as these children were concerned, this was their Uncle Dan!

Apache Elementary PTA President Lauri DeNooy discovered Uncle Dan at the Kansas PTA convention. "All children need an Uncle Dan, and so do our parents and teachers," she stated, matter-of-factly. Lauri invited Uncle Dan to her Title I school. The principal, Mike Weiler, wanted to introduce Uncle

Dan's Report Card in kindergarten through third grades. He had seen the research from our pilot and was impressed.

Although many principals and superintendents knew that there was merit in this program, they had resisted because testing had become the major focus in schools. "Teachers don't need anything else on their plates!" was the mantra of many overwhelmed educators.

"This *is* the plate!" Mr. Weiler said in our first meeting. He understood the research that said when children learn these life skills, they perform better academically. "And this will help our test scores!"

At Apache, Uncle Dan had lunch with each of the eighteen classrooms. After a few minutes to review the habits on his report card, Uncle Dan said, "I am going to ask you a *very big* question. You will have to think very hard and open your minds." Some of the children would open their eyes and mouths extra wide. Some would flair their nostrils and stretch their cheeks. "Here's the big question . . . WHO IS YOUR UNCLE DAN? Who is *another* caring adult, besides me, who teaches you the good habits on my report card?"

Suddenly a few hands shot up. "My mom!" "My grandpa!" "My Uncle Joe!" "My Aunt Dorothy!"

Now everyone's hands reached high. "My neighbor!" "My teacher!" "My coach!" "My big sister!"

"Wowzeeee! Isn't it great! We all have Uncle Dans!"

Uncle Dan is black, white, brown.

He is a she.

Prologue

She is elderly.
He is young.
She is a family member.
He is a role model.
Uncle Dans are everywhere! Everyone can be an Uncle Dan!

> **For more information about the Uncle Dan's Report Card pilot program, please visit UncleDansReportCard.org.**

PART ONE

Raising the Next Great Generation

Back to Basics

The worth of the child cannot be measured in terms of "Per cent" alone. The home life of the child is an important part of the whole life. The teacher's judgment will be a much better one if the home will kindly co-operate. Parents are asked to carefully consider and mark "Home Report" as indicated.

—M. E. PEARSON, SUPERINTENDENT,
KANSAS CITY, KANSAS, PUBLIC SCHOOLS, 1914

Research by "child study" experts of Uncle Dan's day, as well as child development experts and parent-teacher organizations devoted to children's well-being today, all agree that a child needs to believe that her life has value and a sense of purpose in order for her to be successful in school and in life. And Uncle Dan's report card's entries include those Home Habits that have been proven to instill that sense of purpose today, as they did a century ago: to give a child's life worth, to paraphrase Superintendent M. E. Pearson.

These habits were those "purposeful" skills that the school expected the parents to be teaching at home, as we discuss in "1914: Raising Great Citizens" on page 11. The school wanted parents to report how their children were progressing in learning these skills because: "The teacher's judgment will be a much better one if the home will kindly co-operate. Parents are asked to carefully consider and mark 'Home Report' as indicated."

Almost a century later, in 2005, the Association for Supervision and Curriculum Development (ASCD) noted that academic achievement is but one element of student learning and development and only a part of any complete system of educational accountability. ASCD is "accelerating its work to promote the needs of the whole child which recasts the definition of a successful learner from one whose achievement is measured solely by academic tests to one who is knowledgeable, emotionally and physically healthy, civically engaged, prepared for economic self-sufficiency, and ready for the world beyond formal schooling."

So where does this kind of learning begin? In the home, just as it did in 1914. It is the responsibility of the child's caregivers, parents, grandparents, and so on—the child's "Uncle Dans." According to research published by the nonpartisan, nonprofit organization Public Agenda, in 2004, 82 percent of teachers and 74 percent of parents felt that parents' failure to teach their children discipline ranked as one of the biggest causes of school behavior problems.

So here is the foremost challenge for parents and other caregivers in the twenty-first century: to *prioritize* teaching the healthy habits and values on Uncle Dan's report card *at home*, every day, starting in early childhood, with the same emphasis we give to teaching academic subjects at school, every day, starting in early childhood. The words on the back of the 1914 report card still ring true today: "The worth of the child cannot be measured in terms of 'Per cent' alone. The home life of the child is an important part of the whole life."

We believe that the behaviors and values on Uncle Dan's report card are still worthwhile. We believe that we need to teach them to our children and practice them ourselves, just as our grandparents and great-grandparents did for their children, whom Tom Brokaw called the "Greatest Generation." And we believe that doing so at home can have remarkable results.

We not only *believe* this to be true, we now have research to back up these beliefs! According to the research of our Uncle Dan's Report Card pilot program (available at UncleDans ReportCard.org) conducted by Jesse Graham at the University of Virginia Department of Psychology, after using a revised Uncle Dan's Report Card for just six weeks, parents reported that they noticed a positive change in their children's manners, doing chores, hygiene, promptness, organization, reading, screen-time management, meals, and sleep habits. At the same time, Graham's research found that teachers noticed improved behavior, manners, and rule following among those students in families using Uncle Dan's Report Card.

So here we are, bringing Uncle Dan's Report Card to everyone, wherever they live, in order to give everyone the opportunity to pass these "Home Habits" on to their children.

Before we get into the report card chapters and explain how to encourage practicing the behaviors on the Home Report, we want to assure you that this is not an exercise in nostalgia and simply a book about "the good old days."

We know that healthy children then, as healthy children now, behave in essentially the same way children always have. They follow a developmental path from birth through adulthood that is predetermined and hardwired; and it dictates what they understand and how they operate in their worlds. We know generally when children will learn to walk, talk, read, become adolescents, and seek freedom from parents; and we know these scheduled events happen in all children at about the same time. What varies, however, is the context each child finds himself in, the culture of the family and the community.

We also know that children then, as children now, needed structure, rules, routine, and boundaries to feel secure and calm. Not having rules by which to navigate the world in a civilized manner creates anxiety and a sense of chaos, internally and in the culture. No one knows whether to stop or go through the intersection, so to speak, if they don't have a traffic light to give them direction.

Finally, we know that children want to please the people who take care of them and follow their examples, learning what is important in the world from understanding what is important to them.

Thousands of children today, from infancy on, spend more time with teachers, coaches, tutors, and day care workers than with their parents. In 1914, when raising children was a community-wide effort, children were generally expected to work hard and take personal responsibility for themselves. Our research taught us that most people in the 1914 community were on the same page in terms of child rearing. Today, parents, grandparents, and other caregivers often claim to be at a loss as to what to do with their children. They don't know how to set rules, to demand hard work, and to encourage their children to take responsibility, and be accountable, for their own behavior.

Uncle Dan's report card's commonsense code of conduct used by our grandparents and great-grandparents to raise the Greatest Generation is a code of conduct that is just as relevant today. Children are the same—they need structure—and parents are the same, too—they need a set of rules to teach. By emphasizing and encouraging the regular practice of habits such as having good manners, doing homework, and respecting others, Uncle Dan's Report Card fosters a sense of responsibility and personal accountability in children that will improve their performance at school and in their adult life.

Think of the members of your family, teachers, friends, or mentors who were born between 1900 and 1920 or so, as was Uncle Dan, who were taught these habits. In his book *The Greatest Generation*, Tom Brokaw describes them this way:

A sense of personal responsibility and a commitment to honesty is characteristic of this generation. Those were values bred into the young men and women coming of age at the time the war broke out. It's how they were raised. . . . Moreover, in their communities there were always monitors outside of their own families to remind them of the ethos of their family and community. I've always said I was raised by the strict standards of my mother and father, and also of the parents of my friends, my teachers, my coaches, my ministers, and by the local businessmen who didn't hesitate to remind me "that's not how you were raised."

Happily, we discovered Uncle Dan's report card to guide today's parents in educating children by rules that will help them grow up secure, civilized, and motivated to succeed to become part of the next great generation. Children cannot learn or think in a chaotic environment, research shows, and these rules will help them navigate the world with a sense of routine and structure that is practical and positive.

The culture of 1914 seemed to have a moral imperative—an understood urgency—that told children that a good life could be gained through hard work, personal responsibility. and a desire to sacrifice for the greater good. On the other hand, the culture for today's children emphasizes filling every minute with entertainment, blaming others for any failures, and working only for personal gain.

Our task in this book is to take one aspect of the 1914 culture—the universal belief that the goal of parenting is to help children become self-sufficient, responsible adults by modeling and practicing healthy habits and values—and apply it to today's children. A look back at how the Greatest Generation was raised a hundred years ago helps us believe that:

- ✏ Children and their parents, as well as society as a whole, can be successful if children are guided to work hard for what they get.

- ✏ All succeed when children learn to take responsibility for their actions, so that they can suffer the consequences of mistakes they make, and correct those mistakes.

- ✏ Everyone succeeds when children learn the habit of looking out for the welfare of all as they strive to better themselves, to feel the pain of those less fortunate, and to try to ease that pain when possible.

We know that making these beliefs a moral imperative and integrating them as part of one's personal character can produce a society that can overcome great adversity. We know that converting this moral imperative into action can make a generation of great women and men that are motivated to make a great society. We know that when people have a cause they believe in, they will move Heaven and Earth to achieve their goal.

We now have our new cause. So into school district vaults, research libraries, microfilm collections, and the Internet we have gone, to time-travel back to the America, city, school, and home of Uncle Dan's childhood. What we discovered was an America going through tremendous change. Historians call this period the Progressive Era. Reformers pushed for changes that would affect both the school and home life. They helped instill the healthy habits of Uncle Dan's report card because of a new priority placed on children: educating the whole child became the central work of society! Times may have changed, but the importance of the values emphasized in Uncle Dan's report card has not. Now a new generation of parents may be inspired by the work of these reformers of the past to center their children's home life around leadership through the teaching and practicing of these skills every day, in order to raise the Next Great Generation.

1914: Raising Great Citizens

To educate a man in mind and not in morals is to educate a menace to society.

—THEODORE ROOSEVELT,
26TH PRESIDENT OF THE UNITED STATES, 1901–1909

Why was the Home Report developed by Uncle Dan's school district in 1914? As we dug deeper into the national and local history of the time when Dan received his fifth-grade report card, we discovered just how profoundly American society was reflected in the Home Report. It was easy to see how Uncle Dan's report card, with its unique dual reports for School and Home, was the result of new interest in the "science" of parenting, a new spirit of cooperation between home and school, and the desire for European immigrants to adopt American values.

Daniel Leon Brenner, age ten (left), in 1914,
with his younger brother, Harry, age seven.

The New Interest in the "Science" of Parenting

One of the most influential books of the time was *The Century of the Child*, by Ellen Key. Published in 1900, it became an international bestseller. Key proposed that children should be society's first priority during the twentieth century. Key's writings, echoing the principles of Uncle Dan's report card, promoted that society pay attention to the whole child and that the home, rather than the school, begin to play a larger role in child rearing:

Instead of the study of preparation at home for the school taking up, as it now does, the best part of a child's life, the school must get the smaller part, the home the larger part. The home will have the responsibility of so using the free time as well on ordinary days as on holidays, that the children will really become a part of the home both in their work and in their pleasures.

So how did Key's primary emphasis on children in "the home" reflect America's new priority on the *study* of raising children? The topic was a central theme on the agenda of one of the first meetings of the National Congress of Mothers Convention in Washington, DC, in 1899. The program featured Dr. L. Emmett Holt, who pioneered a new generation of male parenting experts in the systematic vocation of child rearing. Holt's *Care and Feeding of Children*, published in 1894, became the parenting bible for mothers that provided the basis for millions of Infant Care Bulletins issued by the Federal Children's Bureau between 1914 and 1921.

Dr. G. Stanley Hall, who was the first PhD in child psychology, was also on the program of the 1899 convention. Hall was a leader in the Child Study Movement in the 1890s, encouraging scientists, parents, and teachers to collect data on every aspect of a child's life. Each of these groups took its role in raising children seriously, and hoped these studies would show the way to teaching good etiquette and values. Between

1894 and 1915, Hall developed hundreds of study questionnaires for children, parents, and teachers. According to *Advances in Child Development and Behavior*, Vol. 17, the topics these questionnaires covered were:

1. Characteristic thoughts and behaviors of young children

2. Children's ethical and religious impulses

3. Problems of childhood ranging from the disciplinary to the psychiatric

4. Children's responses to school settings and activities

5. Professional concerns of educators

We're fairly certain that Uncle Dan's mother, Tillie, did not attend this 1899 convention, but the organization, which later became the National Congress of Mothers and Parent-Teacher Associations, would eventually come to her. In 1914, the year of Uncle Dan's report card, the Kansas Congress of Parents and Teachers was formed as a state branch of the national organization, which later became known as the National PTA.

With many parents of the day engaged in the study and evaluation of their children's behaviors, it is not surprising that Uncle Dan's report card included a Home Report! School district reports of the time show that Uncle Dan's educators were also in support of this national movement being part of their school district.

In her 1911 report for the Board of Education of Kansas City, Kansas, for example, Martha Colton, principal of Long-fellow School, noted that the study of the child was "the first and most important study for both mother and teacher." She reported to the community the fact that child study, was, in her words, "largely American in its origin, and the chief movement both in psychology and education of the nineteenth century."

The New Spirit of Cooperation Between Home and School

Who was leading this forward-thinking school district in the middle of the country? The superintendent of Dan's school district was M. E. Pearson, whose work on the national level to encourage home–school cooperation is convincing evidence that he was the creator of the Home Report.

In 1913, Pearson led two sessions of "The Individual Child and His Individual Needs" at the Fifty-Second Annual Convention of the National Education Association. The first session was subtitled "The School Life of the Child," followed by "The Home Life of the Child." Was the Home Report among the handouts distributed to the session's participants? We found the program note below to be so Pearsonesque:

> It is the purpose of this program to make the individual need of the child the central thought of the department.

Practical school people, with a real live message, will
present the school viewpoint in the school program for
the first session. The home side in the second session
will be given by those not directly connected with the
schools but who have the burdens of child welfare on
their heart and who have much experience in societal
and child welfare programs.

Uncle Dan's report card reflects Pearson's passion for this
home–school cooperative support of children, as do his writings to his fellow educators. In one of his reports to the Board
of Education, Pearson noted that the child should be the focus
of his school district's boards of education, supervisory offices,
and teachers, as well as parents, for one central reason: so that
each child would cooperatively become a better citizen of a
better country.

His enthusiasm for this mission was contagious! Throughout the writings from various educators who worked under
Pearson, the home–school connection was center stage. One
principal wrote: "It is only by the interested, harmonious
working together of home and school that misunderstandings
can be cleared away and ideal conditions be made to exist."

It's interesting to observe that 100 years ago, educators believed that both parents and teachers had to work hard or
"comparatively little could be accomplished" for the welfare of
children. This priority placed on home–school collaboration
wasn't an unspoken assumption. The school district openly

expressed their conviction in "The Twenty-Fifth Annual Report of the Board of Education of the City of Kansas City, Kansas, for the Year July 1, 1910, to June 30, 1911." As we uncovered this document in the stacks of the school district archives, these powerful words gave us goose bumps:

> The two greatest factors in the life of a child are the home and the school. The parents as the representative of the home, and the teacher as the representative of the school, both have a desire to serve the best interests of the child. Each should be able to give him something not obtained from the other. If only one labors, the other remaining indifferent, comparatively little can be accomplished.

Amazing! Then this statement expressed a sense of duty: "This idea of knowledge of the individual, should extend to all questions which concern the health and well-being of pupils," wrote one principal. "It is our duty to know which child is nervous, which nearsighted, and in all cases make due allowances and then remedy in such degree as possible."

To these educators, it was their responsibility to turn to the parents as the "best authority upon the problems of health, proper ideals, and intuitions of the child." They took this responsibility seriously, attributing mistakes in "school management" to the failure of the teacher to comprehend the significance of this responsibility.

The New Immigrants' Adopting of American Values

Pearson's overarching goal of the Home Report—to help each student "become a better citizen of a better country"—was compounded by the cultural diversity of the growing number of immigrants in Kansas City in 1914. The population was estimated at over 91,000. Like most urban areas, it was home to quickly expanding immigrant neighborhoods. Here was where the Irish, Serbians, Croatians, Slovenians, Russians, Germans, Poles, African Americans, Mexicans, and Jews settled. The 1915 census showed that 13.5 percent of Kansas City residents were foreign-born and 11.5 percent were of mixed parentage, "that is whose father or mother were foreign born."

So was the Home Report also one of M. E. Pearson's tactics for getting the culturally diverse families in his district on the same page when it came to instilling the children with the same values and healthy habits? Some literature from the early 1900s makes it seem highly likely because public schools played a pivotal role in the movement to accomplish these goals, a movement called "Americanization."

A document titled "Program for Americanization," published at the time by the business and educational leaders of Kansas City, Kansas, revealed a belief that the public school was "the greatest Americanization force in operation." The authors noted that children had greater influence over their parents than anyone else and brought home the aspects of American culture that they learned in school. Imagine the significance of students bringing home the Home Report with the nineteen behaviors that the school considered important in the home life of the children to help them become great citizens.

It is interesting to note that the cultural differences facing classrooms in 1914 sometimes became sources of unrest within schools. According to Steven Mintz, author of *Huck's Raft*, conflict resulted when native-born teachers had little tolerance for their immigrant pupils. Instead of focusing on the differences between his school families and his staff, however, Pearson made it his mission to bring the home and school together around healthy habits and values that led to success in school and in life. He created a Home Report that was a clear, practical, and effective way to positively send parents his message of the expectations of health and well-being coming from the school, expectations that would lead their children to become "better citizens of a better country."

Whether to collaborate with parents or to help immigrants, or both, it was clear that M. E. Pearson was also totally committed to the development of the whole child, particularly a child's health and well-being. This excerpt from his "Superintendent's Address to the Teachers Before the Opening of Schools, September 9, 1911" reinforced lessons of "rules" about grooming, including caring for teeth and clothes, both of which appeared on the Home Report:

There must be less teaching of the subject and a greater regard for the mental, moral and physical need of the individual child. . . . There must be less mass teaching and more individual application. . . . In many cases it will be necessary to have the children better clothed, housed and groomed. There must be less of nickel shows and exciting entertainment. The physical child must be better cared for. His teeth should be brushed, filled or removed. He must have his tonsils tested and his adenoids taken care of. He must have more protection from contagious diseases and more care in the keeping of his body.

Turning his schools in the early 1900s into places where children learned "means to grace," as he put it, Pearson instructed his teachers to emphasize more than "Per cent" alone. The result was a report card that is a window into the lives of American families in and out of school, families who were inextricably linked together to foster the greater good of America through a new crop of children who became eager to learn what it meant to be proud, hardworking, and responsible citizens of their new country.

> **The worth of the child cannot be measured in terms of "Per cent" alone.**

PART TWO

The Home Report

If you are a parent, recognize that it is the most important calling and rewarding challenge you have. What you do every day, what you say and how you act, will do more to shape the future of America than any other factor in America.

—MARION WRIGHT EDELMAN, FOUNDER, CHILDREN'S DEFENSE FUND

Using This Book

Just as a teacher has her curriculum and guide to teaching that curriculum, you now have a guide to teaching the basic home habits of parenting. As one parent said, "With this book, I know what to do every day to be a good mom. And just like in school, I can track how my child is progressing in these subjects, too."

If you want to give your child every opportunity to succeed in school and in life, you must incorporate these lessons into the rhythm of your family. If you want him to grow up with these habits as part of his character, you must become his Uncle Dan, model these behaviors, and talk about them at every chance. Share this book with others who care for him—all of his Uncle Dans—his teachers, coaches, grandparents, babysitters, etc.

Uncle Dan's Report Card is designed to give you helpful tips to motivate your child to practice each behavior through the "how to teach" section in each chapter. The "takeaways" offer research-based tidbits that explain why this behavior leads to success in school and in life.

As your child grows, you will be helping him learn these behaviors through using the "how to teach" section every day in the normal course of each day. Different behaviors may be more difficult for a child to learn when he is six, but by the time he's ten, he may have them down. Your home is an ongoing class in these subjects, and *Uncle Dan's Report Card* is your "teacher's guide." Just like a child needs to be taught math every day at school, he also needs to be taught habits of kindness every day at home.

One important note: As you use each chapter, keep in mind your child's inborn temperament. Since the 1950s, many scientific studies of temperament have continued to show that a child's abilities to develop and behave appropriately are greatly influenced by the adults in their lives trying to identify, recognize, and respond to their child's unique temperament, in particular. See where your child fits in these broad definitions of Temperament Types below. Keep in mind that approximately 65 percent of all children fit one of three patterns: 40 percent are generally regarded as "easy or flexible"; 10 percent are regarded as "difficult, active, or feisty"; and the final 15 percent are regarded as "slow to warm up or cautious." The other 35 percent of children are a combination of these patterns.

By understanding these patterns, you can best understand your child's ability to learn certain habits and change your approach in such areas as expectations, encouragement, and discipline to fit your child's unique needs.

Temperament Types

- Easy or flexible children are generally calm, happy, adaptable, and not easily upset.

- Difficult, active, or feisty children are often fussy, fearful of new people and situations, easily upset by noise and commotion, high-strung, and intense in their reactions.

- Slow to warm up or cautious children are relatively inactive and fussy, and tend to withdraw or to react negatively to new situations.

The Do's and Don'ts of Using Uncle Dan's Report Card

What to Do

Think about your child's temperament and respect his uniqueness. Do not compare him to others or try to change your child's basic temperament.

Be aware of your own temperament. Adjust your natural responses when they clash with your child's responses.

Communicate with your child. Explain decisions and motives. Listen to your child's points of view and encourage teamwork on generating solutions.

Be a good role model. Children learn by watching and listening to you . . . their "Uncle Dan."

Be sensitive to your child's feelings. Putting yourself in your child's shoes and looking at the subjects from her perspective will help you use kindness and empathy as you work together to learn the habits on Uncle Dan's Report Card.

Be flexible. When your child finds it hard to practice subjects on Uncle Dan's Report Card, think of ways to motivate her that use her strengths rather than point out her weaknesses. Help her understand that mistakes are an inevitable part of life and can be used to find new ways to solve problems.

Keep your anger in check. When children are faced with a parent's anger, they learn to make themselves angry, lose their ability to feel empathy, and fail to learn how to manage their behavior. We make ourselves angry by telling ourselves that our child should do what we want; we don't control our children's behavior, however, just our reaction to it.

Help your child learn that work comes before pleasure. To encourage practicing the subjects on Uncle Dan's Report Card, play "Let's Make a Deal." Here's how it works. Tell your child, "When you have done what you have to do, then you may do what you want to do." Note that it's a positive contract with your child that helps her see the positive consequences of accomplishing goals.

What Not to Do

Don't shame. Shaming will make her feel angry, resentful, and guilty and tells her that your love is conditional. You're teaching her to put others down when they don't live up to her expectations.

Don't bribe. You want to teach your child to meet his responsibilities before doing what he wants, which helps him develop internal motivation. Bribery, on the other hand, teaches your child the opposite. It teaches him to hold out for a tangible payoff before cooperating, keeping his motivation external and dependent on the size of the payoff.

Don't use guilt. Guilt diminishes your child's ability to accept making mistakes. Suggesting that he's flawed sends the erroneous message that his behavior defines who he is.

Don't threaten. Threatening models bullying and decreases her motivation to do what you ask.

Don't label. Don't label your child with negative terms, such as irresponsible, unkind, or lazy. Labeling tells him he is the label and leaves no room for change. Your child isn't his behavior. Always value him; it's his behavior you want to change.

Don't punish. Punishment drives behavior out of sight, not out of existence; it emphasizes what hasn't been done, rather than teaches what to do. Telling your child that he causes your anger diminishes his ability to empathize and makes him believe that he has tremendous power over your emotions. In reality, you're the only one who controls your feelings.

Don't nag. Nagging encourages your child to feel dependent on you and doesn't teach him self-sufficiency. Rather than teaching your child to wait to be told what to do, help him anticipate the subjects on the Report Card and plan to take care of them before doing other activities.

HABIT ONE

Books Read

Every home . . . should contain a library consisting of books suitable for children of all ages. . . . A safe rule for mother is to give her children only books that depict natural lives and point to good morals.

—THE MOTHERS' BOOK: SUGGESTIONS REGARDING
THE MENTAL AND MORAL DEVELOPMENT OF CHILDREN,
BY CAROLINE BENEDICT BURRELL, 1909

Why "Books Read" Mattered Then

Making "Books Read" the first of the nineteen habits makes sense for a community helping its immigrants master the English language.

In *Huck's Raft*, Steven Mintz refers to the period between 1865 and 1910 as "the golden age of American children's fiction." Published in 1914 for Dan and brother Harry to check out from the library was *Tarzan of the Apes*, by Edgar Rice Burroughs. Sisters Babe and Jo would have loved the year's bestseller, *Pollyanna*, by Eleanor H. Porter.

Uncle Dan's mother, Tillie, and the other parents could turn to their school district's growing library system for "books suitable." As the district's library system grew to more than 50,000 titles, the children's librarian made sure to prepare reading lists and suggest books that parents should purchase for their home library. This helps explain Uncle Dan's lifelong love of reading. When he was into his nineties, his home library contained not only classics, but also the latest bestsellers, fiction and nonfiction alike.

Why "Books Read" Matters Today

In order to master any skill, practice is crucial; so to enhance reading ability, there is nothing better than reading books. This is what was believed in 1914 when Uncle Dan was in fifth grade, and it is still true today.

Today, however, children live in a hyperactive world with constant activity and stimulation. Quiet time has disappeared to be replaced by the noise of television, music, electronic beeps, and video games, all competing for the child's attention. As a consequence, children have learned to be hyper-alert and have acquired short attention spans. When a child's brain is craving constant stimulation, it is difficult for the brain to slow down to the leisurely pace required to convert written words into images.

Many classrooms today have requirements for outside reading, but the children need parents who make the time for reading and encourage their children to make lists of books read, just as Uncle Dan's fifth-grade report card did in 1914.

HOW TO TEACH A CHILD TO READ BOOKS

✏ **Make time for daily reading.** To motivate children to read, set aside at least 30 minutes daily for quiet reading time. During that time, cell phones, TVs, radios, iPods, and all other electronic devices are off. Although you've set aside time for reading, the amount of reading done is counted by pages read. To ensure the pages were actually read, ask your child questions about the material.

✏ **Be an Uncle Dan.** During quiet reading time, parents need to be reading also. Children will value reading when they see their parents reading at the same time. Devoting 30 minutes a day to reading models good reading habits for your child.

✏ **Post a list of books read.** We all like to see what we've accomplished for our effort, so put the list on the refrigerator or some other prominent place so your child can count the number of books she has read.

✏ **Praise, praise, praise.** When you see your child reading, compliment him. Praise motivates us to continue to make the effort.

✏ **Go to the library with your child and encourage her to check out books for her to read or for you to read to her.** Ask your child's teacher for recommended books that will help your child's reading skills develop at a level appropriate for her.

Schools that used Uncle Dan's Report Card increased parents' ratings of children's habits regarding chores, hygiene, promptness, organization, manners, reading, meals and sleep habits in just a six-week period.

—DIRECTOR OF RESEARCH FOR
UNCLE DAN'S REPORT CARD
KANSAS PILOT PROGRAM

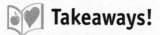 **Takeaways!**

- Anne Henderson's research at the University of Michigan found that the following factors enhance school success: encouraging reading and discussion by reading to children, listening to them read, discussing what's being read, telling stories, and writing stories.

- Research into the effects of TV viewing on education found that first graders who watched more than seven hours of TV a week in their preschool years earned lower grades than those who watched less. Further, TV suppressed reading ability by directly exciting the brain with images, rather than requiring the brain to translate printed words into images.

- The joy of reading will encourage your child to love books as she grows. By having one-on-one reading time with each of your children, you can discover if a child is having difficulty seeing the words (does she need glasses?), hearing your voice read the words (does her hearing need testing?), or sounding out words (is there a comprehension problem?). Check with your child's teacher or health care provider if you're concerned.

Letters Written

The ability to write rapidly and legibly is still important. Outside the school both children and adults write various types of letters. They also make valuable records of such matters as experiences, minutes, recipes, sales and the like. . . . One more point should be mentioned here. Teaching the use of the typewriter has been proposed as a substitute for instruction in handwriting. . . . Most parents cannot afford to buy them for children, and at the present time school boards are not in position to supply them gratis in adequate numbers. Apparently there is no way out, and some time or other the child must learn to write by hand.

—*LANGUAGE IN THE ELEMENTARY SCHOOL: COMPOSITION, SPELLING, AND WRITING,*
BY PAUL MCKEE, PHD, 1939

Why "Letters Written" Mattered Then

Letter writing gave Uncle Dan and his classmates an opportunity to practice their penmanship, which was a point of emphasis in the Board of Education Reports of the time.

During his fifth-grade year, Dan wrote a total of only five letters, according to his Home Report. Perhaps this is why as an attorney and a judge, he was not known for having easy-to-read handwriting. Those of us who tried to read his handwriting doubt that Dan received the Superintendent's Honorary Rank stamp from Superintendent Pearson given "when a child has made satisfactory improvement at the end of the year." Yet it always felt special to receive a handwritten letter or thank-you note from Uncle Dan!

It is interesting to note that the following abilities, which were featured in *Language in the Elementary School: Composition, Spelling and Writing*, were considered to be "among those peculiar to letter-writing":

- A realization that a letter is a means of communication.

- A realization that a letter has different parts.

- A sensitivity to the situation in which a letter should be written.

- A knowledge of the purpose of each of the different parts of a letter (heading, salutation, body, ending, and signature).

- The ability to capitalize, punctuate, and place correctly the heading, salutation, ending, and signature.

- A knowledge of the relative position of each of the parts of the letter.

- A knowledge of what should be included in each part of a letter.

- The ability to space the various parts of a letter properly.

✏ A knowledge of the appropriateness of different types of salutations, addresses, and endings in terms of the addresses and the type of letter being written.

✏ A knowledge of what is appropriate to say in a letter in terms of the circumstances of the writing.

Also outlined were the "Attitudes essential to good practice," including:

✏ Answering the questions that have been asked.

✏ Implying or expressing respect and esteem.

✏ Expressing earned congratulations.

✏ Expressing sympathy when needed.

✏ Expressing good wishes.

✏ Mailing letter promptly.

✏ Not writing letters in anger.

✏ Answering letters with relative promptness.

Considering the forms of communication today that have taken the place of letter writing, including emails, texts, and tweets, it's easy to see how much care was placed on how people treated one another, even in print, a century ago, compared to how we casually "speak" in writing today.

Why "Letters Written" Matters Today

In today's world of instant communication, letter writing seems incredibly slow and laborious. Handwriting has fallen into disuse with typing and texting taking its place. Some schools are considering doing away with teaching cursive writing to children. More time now is spent keyboarding than handwriting.

With the decline in handwritten letters, children and adults have turned to email and texting to condense the time it takes to share thoughts. By email or text, snippets can be exchanged quickly; but what about the narrative, punctuation, and spelling? Letter writing teaches children critical thinking skills—how to clarify and support thoughts and arguments in ways that emailing or texting doesn't. Because of the brevity expected in a text message or email, both the sender and the recipient may be more likely to quickly exchange thoughts without paying attention to expressing themselves clearly, explaining their own feelings, or considering how their words will affect others. What about the emotion told through handwriting style? Emails and text messages can be misinterpreted as curt and cold, owing to their terse and shorthand style. Never underestimate the timeless power of a long and heartfelt handwritten thank-you note or love letter!

The practice of letter writing will hone a child's skills in written communication, which can improve every aspect of his academic and professional life: grade school and high school reports, term papers, college application essays, and business letter writing, for example. His love of letter writing could spark an interest in a career in creative writing or business communications! If he becomes a good letter writer, a child will be even better wherever he communicates—online or on paper.

HOW TO TEACH A CHILD TO WRITE LETTERS

☞ **Make writing a requirement.** Sit down each night with your child and help her to compose a letter to a friend or relative that tells something about his thoughts, feelings, and aspirations. Once the requirement is put in place, your child will begin thinking about the day's events so she can have something to write; and reviewing the day helps her reflect on and learn from her daily experiences. Doing so also helps her develop the habit of expressing her emotions with you.

☞ **Be an Uncle Dan.** Renew your own letter-writing skills by sitting with your child, so you can write together. When she sees you writing, the act of writing becomes more important.

☞ **Praise, praise, praise.** Compliment your child's writing by focusing on the effort put into the activity rather than on the product. Say, for example, "You must have worked hard on this. Hard work can result in really good writing."

☞ **When you have . . . then you may.** Keeping distractions away and holding TV, video games, cell phones, and computers until the writing assignment has been done will motivate your child. To ensure quality, have corrections of spelling and grammar made before the assignment is considered complete.

————

I wish I had been able to have Uncle Dan's Report Card when I was a child!

—PARENT OF A PRESCHOOLER, UNCLE DAN'S
REPORT CARD KANSAS PILOT PROGRAM

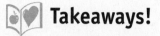 **Takeaways!**

- Use expressions of thankfulness to help your child gain practice in writing. If he is too young to write, ask him to draw "thank-you" pictures to express his affection to you, his teachers, or other family members.

- Always require the writing of "thank-you" notes when you child receives a gift, has been invited to a party, or has been a guest. Doing so helps him get in touch with his feelings as well develop his letter-writing and social skills.

Hours Worked

Children began to work less toward the end of the nineteenth century. A rising tide of economic, humanitarian, and even evolutionary writings opposed child labor. . . . The 1870 census found one in eight children between 10 and 15 employed. By 1900, there were one out of six employed. By 1918, all states had compulsory school attendance laws and 17 enforced child labor laws.

—*ADVANCES IN CHILD DEVELOPMENT AND BEHAVIOR*, VOL. 17,
EDITED BY HAYNE W. REESE, 1982

Why "Hours Worked" Mattered Then

The habits "Hours Worked," "Money Earned," "Helping Mother," and "Helping Father" were entwined for many parents in 1914 Kansas City, Kansas.

Viviana Zelizer, author of *Pricing the Priceless Child*, explains why:

As twentieth-century American children became defined by their sentimental, noneconomic value, child work could no longer remain "real" work; it was only justifiable as a form of education or as a sort of game. The useful labor of the nineteenth century child was replaced by educational work for the useless child. While child labor had served the household economy, child work would benefit primarily the child.

According to an 1894 article in the magazine *The Industrialist*, home work for boys would include sawing wood; tending gardens and furnaces; taking caring of livestock and business offices; cleaning windows; selling milk, papers, and novelties; and working on farms during vacation. "Let the work be difficult while it lasts, but avoid placing the boy to work in the midst of evil influences."

Dan's parents recorded zeros across the "Hours Worked" row, probably because Dan did not have a job outside the home. With many children working outside the home, and many dropping out of school to work full time to help support the family, zeros would be a positive sign to Dan's teacher that Tillie and Adolph were serious about keeping Dan in school. This goal may have been a challenge for many immigrant families who relied on their children to contribute to the family economy in the "Old Country." The row below labeled "Money Earned" showed that Dan earned money, which was probably paid to him by his parents as an allowance for helping around the house or the store.

As children's work became more confined to the home, schools adapted to place more emphasis on the child's contributions to the household. In *Pricing the Priceless Child*, Zelizer noted:

To help parents navigate through these changing attitudes toward child labor, one progressive Birmingham school introduced a parents' report card "to help the child by recognizing industry and excellence in home occupations." Parents were asked to grade as satisfactorily, excellent, fairly good, unsatisfactory, ordinary, or very poor a wide range of domestic activities performed by their children, such as garden work, care of household tools, care of furnace, making fires, care of horse or cow, sweeping and dusting, making beds, and general cooking.

Perhaps this parents' report card was the inspiration for M. E. Pearson's Home Report! It, too, included "care of clothing," "making things," and "interest in books."

Why "Hours Worked" Matters Today

The same fuzzy line between "Hours Worked," "Money Earned," "Helping Mother," and "Helping Father" of 1914 still exists today. Because working—whether that means doing homework, chores, or helping others—has been proven to help children become useful citizens and believe that their lives have "worth," it is important for parents to "put their children to work" at home or outside the home.

As in the case of adults, all children can be motivated to work by their desire to receive three internal "rewards":

- Personal pleasure from working for the greater good with the welfare of everybody in mind, rather than just personal welfare (intrinsic)

- Accomplishing a goal to achieve a meaningful outcome, rather than simply achieving some material gain

- Taking responsibility for one's own behavior, being accountable to oneself for doing a job to the best of one's ability, without blaming others for mistakes or shortcomings

Helping your child value "work" because of these intrinsic rewards is a goal for every parent. With that internal motivation to "do the right thing," your child will practice these behaviors until they become a habit, and these habits will become their character.

Of course, wanting to earn money to help the family budget or to purchase things that they want can be healthy "external" motivation for spending hours at work! Monitoring the time spent "working for pay" outside the home and the amount of "work" spent on schoolwork is important today, as it was a century ago. Only you and your family can know what is in the best interests of everyone.

In either case, developing a healthy work ethic will lead to lifelong success in the adult world of independent, self-sufficient, self-reliant living.

HOW TO TEACH A CHILD TO VALUE WORK

✏ **Find jobs at home that children can do.** If you are currently outsourcing housecleaning, turn the tasks over to your children. A few hours each week could be devoted to vacuuming, scrubbing floors and bathrooms, and helping with yard work. Set the goals for your child, so she can experience the good feelings that come from accomplishing a task. Let her know how much her work means to the family's welfare, so she realizes that she can make a difference by being helpful.

✏ **Be an Uncle Dan.** Showing children how to work is essential because the visual model of how to accomplish a job is a better teaching tool than just telling them what to do. Children also need to see you working as the model for how to work. Taking your children to work can also be helpful, so they can see you on your job. Plan to do that on school holidays or during summer vacation, so the children won't miss any school.

✏ **Praise, praise, praise.** Praising your child's effort will go far in teaching him that the process of working is more valuable than the outcome of work. It's the trip that's worthwhile, not the destination.

Because of Uncle Dan's Report Card, we had more parents at parent-teacher conferences than ever before!

—ELEMENTARY SCHOOL TEACHER, UNCLE DAN'S
REPORT CARD KANSAS PILOT PROGRAM

Takeaways!

- Motivate your child to be accountable for completing jobs in a timely manner. Say, for example, "When you have finished the vacuuming and I've inspected it, then you may have your cell phone back." This "inspection" communicates accountability, a motivation for young and old alike missing in today's culture.

- Look for mentors who can help guide your child toward practicing a good work ethic on schoolwork, homework, or in doing jobs inside or outside the home.

- Watch your words. Children are listening to our attitudes, as well as our actions. Observe just how much you complain about your job, for example, which can communicate to your little ones that work is not something that is supposed to be enjoyable. "Work" has a different meaning to each person: to some, homework is "work"; to others, simply answering emails is "work." What you say will go a long way in influencing how children define "work," including "schoolwork" and the jobs they take on inside or outside the home . . . for love or money!

HABIT FOUR

Money Earned

Ironically, once children were removed from the market, their home became a place of employment. After all, if parents were one of the few remaining legitimate employers, where else could the child earn money?

—*PRICING THE PRICELESS CHILD: THE CHANGING SOCIAL VALUE OF CHILDREN,*
BY VIVIANA ZELIZER, 1985

Why "Money Earned" Mattered Then

Tillie reported Dan's earnings for each six-week period: $1.00, $2.00, $3.00, $1.00, $1.00 . . . Uncle Dan was a productive earner for a fifth grader!

Yet it is likely that many of Dan's classmates earned money from jobs outside the home out of economic necessity or for spending money. "Most immigrant families depended on children's labor, whether this involved childcare, shopping, cooking, scavenging in the streets, or paid work inside or outside the home. Low wages made income pooling necessary. A federal study found that only 20 percent of Jewish immigrant fathers in seven major cities could support their families on their earnings," according to Steven Mintz, author of *Huck's Raft.*

One study at the time asked children between the third and eighth grades, "How do you get the money you have to spend?" A majority of the boys and girls said that they earned it. The girls earned money by running errands, doing housework, and baby-sitting. The boys worked for their parents, ran errands, sold papers or ice, caddied, and shined shoes.

Earning their own spending money would teach responsibility and thrift, a concept reinforced by the saying "A fool and his money are soon parted."

Why "Money Earned" Matters Today

Today, parents give children an allowance as a way of providing money to spend, with the hope that they will budget adequately so it will last from week to week. If the child runs out of money, however, she is often able to cajole her parents for additional funds, which teaches children how to badger, wheedle, and beg until exhausted parents give in!

Because there are very few opportunities today for children to earn money outside the home before the age of sixteen, money earned comes from the family budget. Rather than give an allowance, parents can pay their children for their labor within the family; but few parents see the value of paying wages versus giving an allowance.

So let's explore the difference between allowance and

wages. Wages are payments for labor or services according to contract and on an hourly, daily, or piecework basis. An allowance is given without exchange of goods or services as a share or portion allotted or granted as a fixed or available amount. In short, a wage is payment for doing something; an allowance is a grant for doing nothing. Children who earn a wage learn how to work for what they get. Children who depend on an allowance learn to expect money just because they exist.

The question, therefore, becomes one of deciding which is best for children and will help them become useful citizens. In 1914, it was the consensus that children should earn their money as a way to help them value hard work. Today, many parents believe children should be given any money they want, for whatever they want, no strings attached. As a result, today's children have a sense of entitlement, have an inflated self-image, and are overly dependent on their parents.

If you would like your children to value hard work, giving them a no-strings-attached allowance will not accomplish that goal. Paying wages for work accomplished will.

HOW TO TEACH A CHILD TO EARN MONEY

✏ **Make a list of jobs.** Deciding your child's capability is important as you determine what she can do. Small children can't manage the vacuum cleaner, but they can dust. Listing jobs and the amount each job is worth when successfully completed will help your child understand how much she can earn.

- **Show how each job is done.** Children need to be shown, not just told, the proper way to complete each job, which increases the chances it will be done successfully.

- **Avoid giving extra money.** To help your child know that he must depend on his own labor to earn money, don't get trapped into subsidizing activities or letting your child buy on credit. Otherwise, your child doesn't learn to live within a budget.

- **Be an Uncle Dan.** Try to live within your own budget, so you don't overspend, and tell your child what you are doing. "I wish I could buy a new outfit, but that expense doesn't fit in my budget. I'll have to wait until I've earned enough to afford it."

Uncle Dan's Report Card worked better the more I used it.

—PARENT OF A FIRST GRADER, UNCLE DAN'S
REPORT CARD KANSAS PILOT PROGRAM

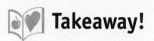 **Takeaway!**

- Overindulged children, who are given all of the material things they want, with no requirements for them to do anything to earn these material possessions, are more likely to grow up self-centered and angry, have low motivation, and lack self-sufficiency.

Money Saved

There is a great deal more said and written about the art of earning than the science of spending, yet one is quite as important as the other. It is not fair to our children to permit them to grow up without any systematic training as to thrift, and then to expect that by some magical process they will become skillful financiers.

—"TEACHING THRIFT," *AMERICAN MOTHERHOOD*,
EMMA GARY WALLACE, 1916

Why "Money Saved" Mattered Then

"There has probably been no aspect of family life which has been the cause of greater strain and stress than the problem of the child and his money," noted Michael V. O'Shea, a professor of education at the University of Wisconsin, in 1915.

William McKeever of Kansas State Agricultural College would agree. In an 1894 article he wrote, "There is no good reason why any ordinary boy should not be taught to work and to save and to have a small bank account of his own, providing he be given reasonable instruction in regard to the matter . . . this instruction will prove in the end to be as profitable in every sense as that given on any other conceivable subject, for it will become a great moral force."

"A penny saved is a penny earned," said Poor Richard's Almanac in 1901. To encourage saving money in 1914, children were given piggy banks or the popular mechanical banks that would perform an action before it swallowed the coin, much to the delight of the child. Because of the arduous work children often had to do to earn the money, saving it was important to them. The harder they worked for the money, the more valuable the money became to the child.

The Home Report shows that Dan saved most of the money he earned. During the first six-week period he saved everything he earned. His savings income dropped during the second period when he earned $2.00 and saved $1.75. All in all, however, he was an impressive saver.

Why "Money Saved" Matters Today

Children are less inclined to save money when they are over-indulged with every material possession they want, including cash. This is true not only because they didn't earn it, but also because money has less value to them. Because of the ability to just pull out a credit card, instead of needing cash to pay for everything, adults are often not in the habit of "paying as they go." This habit can be dangerous as "living within my means" may often mean "living on a borrowed dime." Children see this and think that they, too, can simply buy now and pay later, expecting a parent to always be there to provide additional funds when they run out. Without understanding the importance and value of savings, children are in for a rude awakening as they enter adulthood and discover that money really doesn't grow on trees.

HOW TO TEACH A CHILD TO SAVE MONEY

- **Be an Uncle Dan.** If you want your child to learn about thrift and to save money, you need to model saving for him. Talk out loud as you review your budget, so your child will hear you talk about how much money you are putting into savings each month. Explain to him why you are saving money and what happens when you do.

- **Have your child earn money.** Children who earn their money by working hard are more likely to save it because of the effort they had to expend earning it. Paying for chores completed successfully gives your child a way to earn money.

- **Mandate saving.** Make saving money a requirement by having your child set aside a percentage of his earnings to put into savings. Not only will your child make saving a habit, but he will quickly understand and learn to compute percentages.

- **Review purchases.** When your child wants to buy something with her earnings, require a purchase plan that includes a discussion of the need for the item, the price of the item, a comparison of prices from other vendors, the tax or shipping charges, and the amount left in savings after the purchase.

- **Praise, praise, praise.** Tell your child how much you appreciate his sense of thrift, as he saves his money. Remember to praise the process of saving rather than the outcome, so the act of saving becomes more important.

I've never seen children so happy and excited to talk about good behaviors.

—PTA PRESIDENT OF AN ELEMENTARY SCHOOL,
UNCLE DAN'S REPORT CARD KANSAS PILOT
PROGRAM

Takeaways!

• A 2002 study from the UCLA Center on Everyday Lives of Families found that the typical American family owns more than most Egyptian pharaohs, which results in a scale of consumption the world has never before seen. Teaching saving reduces the need to consume.

• Child development experts found that teaching children to delay gratification improves their ability to focus their attention and accomplish tasks.

• Earning money provides the opportunity to give some of the child's riches to charity. Doing so serves three purposes: helping others, feeling grateful for having enough to share, and sacrificing for the greater good.

HABIT SIX

Things Made

[The child] loves to make things; give it a paste pot, a pair of scissors, a knife, a needle, and see the pleasure it will take in evolving something of its very own . . . through handicraft, it also works off a large part of its superfluous energy, where there is no opportunity for the study of handicraft in a school. Within reason, the father and mother should try to make some opportunity for it at home.

—*THE MOTHERS' BOOK: SUGGESTIONS REGARDING THE MENTAL AND MORAL DEVELOPMENT OF CHILDREN,* BY CAROLINE BENEDICT BURRELL, 1909

Why "Things Made" Mattered Then

Uncle Dan, the adult, was not known as the family handyman. So it is no surprise that a row of zeros spread across the page of his Home Report for "Things Made."

To the educators, "Things Made" was a habit that led to productive members of the labor force. Superintendent Pearson weighed in on the importance of the new movement for manual training:

There was a great movement in education toward a more vital, tangible and practical form of instruction. As an expression of this, manual training became an important factor in every important school system. At first the sole object of manual training was to teach the child to make something with tools. It was then considered more and more that manual training was designed chiefly to bring the child into sympathy with the industrial side of life. Manual training took its place along with other time-honored branches as being an educative process and included more than the handling of tools.

In Uncle Dan's fifth-grade world, store-bought toys were few and far between. Children were encouraged to make things for their own entertainment, including forts made from scrap wood and rocks. Tree houses were made from cast-off lumber and used nails that could be straightened with a hammer. Sailboats were made from pieces of wood, with sticks making masts and paper for sails. If a child was fortunate enough to find a cast-off roller skate, the wheels could be nailed to boards to make a scooter, which would bring hours of fun.

Why "Things Made" Matters Today

In today's world, there seems to be an almost infinite number and variety of toys and games available for children. The design and manufacture of games and toys is big business. And the number of batteries sold now to power the toys must number in the billions, for almost all toys talk, walk, growl, whistle, roar, sing, or beep. Children today want for nothing in the area of entertainment.

Creativity and inventiveness have taken a backseat today to passive entertainment. Toys do the work and the child observes. Much of today's recreation for children at home involves more passive observation than interaction. Video games involve participation by the player and may help children learn rapid decision making and multitasking, but do not require much physical action and certainly don't encourage creativity.

When children make things, from cookies to clay pots, they not only use creativity, but also learn how to follow a project through all of its phases, from beginning to end. Teaching them to complete what they start is an important lesson that will serve them well in successfully mastering school and workplace assignments. During the process of making things, children also get practice in following directions and solving problems, two other habits that they need to develop to be successful. When making things with others, children learn how to collaborate, share, and delegate jobs, all of which will help them in cooperative learning projects at school, teamwork in the workplace, and family relationships.

HOW TO TEACH A CHILD TO MAKE THINGS

- **Provide creative activities.** In order for children to develop their creative potential, art and writing projects that use their artistic talents and toys and games that stimulate their imagination are necessary. Toys that require children to build, invent, design, and manipulate also encourage problem solving.

- **Encourage creativity.** Asking questions—such as, "How could you make one yourself?"—requires your child to think through a process and involves planning and implementation.

- **Be an Uncle Dan.** Show your child how you make things. Creating meals, inventing games, making crafts, knitting a scarf, all demonstrate to your child how to use his mind to open up new possibilities and how good it feels to accomplish a goal.

- **Praise, praise, praise.** When you see your child create something, talk about the work and the ideas involved. Saying, "That's a great idea to use that leftover ribbon to wrap Grandma's gift" not only encourages more creativity but also helps your child think of herself as being creative.

Children who practiced the habits on Uncle Dan's Report Card showed improvements in classroom manners and rule following.

—SECOND-GRADE TEACHER, UNCLE DAN'S REPORT
CARD KANSAS PILOT PROGRAM

Takeaways!

- In a University of Kansas study on the effects of TV on education, it was found that gifted children in fourth, fifth, and sixth grades who watched shows ranging from cartoons to "educational TV" had depressed creativity scores on subsequent testing.

- Many educators believe that the school culture that focuses heavily on achievement testing discourages creative thinking by teaching children that all questions in the world have only one right answer.

- Research indicates that a child's ability to use her imagination may be a bigger factor in predicting academic success than the more traditional measure of aptitude, her intelligence quotient.

- According to the American Academy of Pediatrics, parents need to spend more time playing with their children and focusing on simple old-fashioned toys instead of high-tech ones to build their creative potential.

Evenings at Home

Of all the juvenile discipline suited to inculcate love of home, respect for the family and the fundamental principles of patriotism, the evening hour with the children and parents participating is perhaps the most to be commended. When this occasion is properly managed the business cares of the father are forgotten, the household burdens of the mother are laid aside, while the affairs of the children hold the center of interest.

—"THE EVENING HOUR WITH THE CHILDREN,"
AMERICAN MOTHERHOOD, WILLIAM MCKEEVER, 1917

Why "Evenings at Home" Mattered Then

Dan's parents had Evenings at Home "properly managed." According to their marks on the Home Report, he spent *every* evening at home.

They had some help getting him there. The Kansas City, Kansas, Armour meat packing plant had a big steam whistle that blew every night at nine o'clock. Many families used it as the "curfew" warning, for the children knew that they had better be home when it sounded.

For M. E. Pearson and his staff, "Evenings at Home" was

probably a strategy to save children's lives, both physically and morally. According to *Pricing the Priceless Child*:

By 1910, accidents had become the leading cause of death for children ages five to fourteen. . . . Railroads, streetcars, and automobiles emerged as fiercer killers of children than communicable diseases, which were being rapidly controlled by medical research and improved public health. Between 1910 and 1913, over 40 percent of New York traffic victims were under fifteen years of age. In 1914, the rate jumped to 60 percent.

Evenings at home were also much preferred for boys over evenings spent at the pool hall, which the *Kansas City Kansan* warned about as "a place where they meet the bootlegger, the tinhorn gambler and the agent of the prostitute."

Above all, evenings were considered a special time for families to spend time together. The 1903 book *A Series of Don'ts for Mothers, Who May, or May Not, Stand in Need of Them*, by Gabrielle E. Jackson, advised:

Don't fail to reserve at least one hour of your day for your child's *very own*. Make it and keep it sacred; it pays compound interest.

Why "Evenings at Home" Matters Today

Children today have a tremendous array of evening activities outside the home available to them, all because of the easy access to lighting and transportation. Movies, ball games, shopping malls, and playgrounds are only a few of the possible evening activities. Children are delivered to lessons, sports practices, friends' houses, malls, and myriad other places for evening activities outside the home long into the night. The number of evening activities, along with the access to a wide array of electronic devices that take children's attention away from home and family in the evening, suggest that "Evenings at Home" have a different priority for parents today.

But no matter how difficult it may be to spend evenings at home together, current research makes a convincing argument for doing so, especially around the dinner table. One of the greatest predictors of good behavior and academic achievement in school is the family dinner. Children who eat dinner with the family at least three times a week are better behaved and achieve at a higher level than those who don't. When children have positive interaction with their caring adults, their "Uncle Dans," they learn manners and good social skills. The stimulation of language results in better achievement in school.

HOW TO TEACH A CHILD TO SPEND EVENINGS AT HOME

- **Review your child's schedule.** Children who are overscheduled and find themselves constantly on the go will become stressed, exhausted, and unable to adequately focus on learning. Restrict as many evening activities as possible to free up more time at home.

- **Make evenings at home fun.** Children want to do things that are fun, so schedule time for family games in the evening that encourage talking and listening to each other. Make your evenings at home less stressful by leaving your work at the office and cell phones off.

- **Be an Uncle Dan.** If you are overscheduled, then begin to reduce as many outside demands on your time as possible. If your child sees you going out constantly or doing outside work while at home, then he will think that's the thing for him to be doing.

- **Focus on learning.** Your child's job is to go to school and succeed there. Planning evenings at home that encourage learning and enhance her chances in school is the most important task for you to oversee during the school year.

The Report Card reinforced positive behaviors both at home and at school. I can't wait to use it at home with my teenage children.

—FIRST-GRADE TEACHER AND PARENT OF
TEENAGERS, UNCLE DAN'S REPORT CARD
KANSAS PILOT PROGRAM

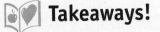 # Takeaways!

- The UCLA Center for Everyday Lives of Families found that because of evenings taken up by lessons and sports, individuals in the family treat each other indifferently, with children not greeting parents when they meet.

- Anne Henderson's research in school success at the University of Michigan found that children's academic performance improves when their parents encourage reading, writing, and discussion in the family. Specific ways to do so include reading to children, listening to them read, discussing what's being read, telling stories, sharing problems, writing letters and stories, and making lists. These activities require families being together at home in the evening.

Care of Teeth

With the increase of medical and dental science, a third problem is demanding a solution by physicians and teachers. This problem is the care of children's teeth. Statistics show that children having poor teeth lose one school year out of every eight. When we consider this loss, the pain and suffering of the children, the poor health caused by faulty mastication and imperfect digestion, we should be deeply impressed with the fact that dental inspection is of vital importance to the boys and girls. Those who have studied this question most carefully maintain that there should be dental inspection with accurate reports to parents. They also request that teachers should give pupils instructions regarding the care of their teeth.

—A REPORT TO THE BOARD OF EDUCATION ON JUNE 30, 1911,
TITLED "HEALTH AND HYGIENE IN THE PUBLIC SCHOOLS,"
BY IDA M. MEYER, PRINCIPAL, PRESCOTT SCHOOL

Why "Care of Teeth" Mattered Then

In 1914, Care of Teeth was such a serious concern for the district that local dentists offered free services to school dental clinics. Lesson 5, "The Teeth," in *Oral Lesson Book in Hygiene for Primary Teachers*, published in 1901, suggested a clever lesson idea to get the students' attention:

Tell them the story of Colonel Roosevelt and his Rough Riders as they went into the battle at El Caney. All the luggage had to be left behind except the mackintoshes (rain gear) which protected the men from the heavy rains, but they needed their toothbrushes so much that they stuck them into their hat bands and carried them in this way rather than go with out them. . . . Form a toothbrush brigade in your own school for each boy and each girl to join who will try to take as good care of their teeth as did this regiment of United States soldiers.

According to *Anxious Parents*, by Peter N. Stearns, tooth-brushing during these times was considered an "unnatural act." The first widely used American dental cream, Dr. Shef-field's Crème Dentifrice, came on the market in 1892, and new kinds of brushes soon followed.

Although the first toothbrush was made in the eighteenth century, they were made with animal bristles and were expensive. Synthetic bristles weren't used until 1938, so Uncle Dan had to brush his teeth with a primitive brush that wasn't often replaced. Tooth powder was preferred by most until around 1917, although toothpaste made from hydrogen peroxide and baking soda was available. Many families relied on a home-made mixture of salt and baking soda because it was cheap and effective.

Why "Care of Teeth" Matters Today

Dental hygiene is still considered important today and has become a big business. Children now have electric toothbrushes, bubblegum-flavored toothpaste, dental floss holders, and chemicals that color the bad stuff on teeth to show what was missed at the last brushing. Dentists specialize in dealing with children, with fun waiting rooms, videos to watch, and a playful chairside manner to offset fears of going to the dentist.

Today's research on tooth decay reveals that the risk of heart disease and cancer can be increased by unhealthy gums. Even with all the advances in tooth care, it's still hard to get children to brush their teeth after each meal as recommended. Tooth brushing isn't fun, and today's child wants everything to be fun. If parents keep in mind their long-term goals for their children, it will motivate them to persevere even in the face of their child's resistance.

HOW TO TEACH A CHILD TO CARE FOR HIS TEETH

- **Be an Uncle Dan.** Brush your teeth while your child is brushing hers. Not only will she learn how it's done, but she'll see that you think it's important enough to brush, too.

- **Praise, praise, praise.** Thanking children for brushing their teeth and telling them how well they are brushing will motivate them to continue good dental hygiene.

✏ **When you have . . . then you may.** Following toothbrushing with reading a favorite story motivates children to get the job done, so story time can begin. Say, "When your teeth are clean, then we can read stories."

✏ **Use a checklist.** To remind older children that toothbrushing is a part of their daily routine, make a checklist that reminds them. Checklists can be very basic: Get up; get dressed; eat breakfast; brush teeth; get books ready for school; wait for the bus. Repeat each day.

———

The flexibility of Uncle Dan's Report Card is its strength.

—COUNSELOR AT AN ELEMENTARY SCHOOL, UNCLE
DAN'S REPORT CARD KANSAS PILOT PROGRAM

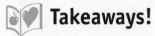 **Takeaways!**

- Soft drinks and sweet fruit juices are the biggest culprits in contributing to tooth decay, gum disease, and obesity. Encourage your child to drink water when thirsty.

- Making teethbrushing a habit means accomplishing this goal every day and taking pride in this accomplishment.

- Use empathy when encouraging children to take care of their teeth. For example, if the dentist you choose for your child is not motivating her to take care of her teeth, try to understand what upsets your child and make changes in practitioner if necessary.

Regular Bathing

As the *New York Times* explained, in 1927, "Have children report on days they take baths at home. The type of home will determine whether to expect more than two baths a week." Children themselves were encouraged to tattle on home conditions as part of the schools' commitment to drive the new standards home.

—*ANXIOUS PARENTS: A HISTORY OF MODERN CHILDREARING IN AMERICA*, BY PETER N. STEARNS, 2004

Why "Regular Bathing" Mattered Then

Hygiene messages and school campaigns in the early twentieth century taught parents that germs were the greatest danger to their children's health and that regular bathing was a key way to combat germs. Not only was it a matter of keeping children healthy, but bathing was also seen as an essential part of respectable personal hygiene habits.

The report from the Fourth International Congress on School Hygiene published in 1914 stated that "if all the population of these broad United States could be made to feel the importance of the bath we could greatly reduce the morbidity" and "if this subject of community hygiene could be put to the child that he could take it to the home there would be a great change for the betterment of each community."

But back in 1914, regular bathing wasn't all fun and games. The kitchen was the warmest place for bathing because of the cookstove, which also heated the water. Because water was not always easily available, several children may have been bathed in the same water. As a result, bathing was an unpleasant chore rather than something to look forward to for many families.

Why "Regular Bathing" Matters Today

Many children still avoid bathing if they can, but not because of lack of privacy, sharing water with siblings, or harsh soap. Today's children don't want to waste their valuable playtime by bathing. To make it easier, parents often fill the bathtub with toys as an enticement for the child, but the child ends up playing with the toys and not bathing himself. Adolescents, on the other hand, bathe or shower often because they fear being rejected by their peers because of offensive body odor.

There may be a problem, however, with bathing too much. Researchers have concluded that too much bathing can rob the body of beneficial oils and bacteria and may weaken children's immune systems. Striking a balance between keeping children clean and giving their bodies a chance to regrow the good bacteria and replenish the oils makes good sense.

Today, regular bathing has taken a backseat to hand hygiene, which is the new cleanliness mandate. The spread of disease is directly attributed to dirty hands, so schools have instituted hand-washing protocols. Children are told to wash their hands while they repeat the alphabet, which takes about fourteen seconds, the time needed to remove germs from the hands.

HOW TO TEACH A CHILD REGULAR BATHING

✏ **Make it routine.** If bathing and hand washing are a part of an established routine, children will find comfort in following the routine. Children like life to be predictable.

✏ **Praise, praise, praise.** Telling children how well they are cleaning their faces or ears can show them you think what they are doing is important.

✏ **Be an Uncle Dan.** When children see you routinely wash your hands and take your bath or shower, they will be more likely to see these as important. To get children to wash hands long enough, make a game out of washing and singing the alphabet song.

———

It is so useful as a tool for talking to my children about the different habits.

—PARENT OF A SECOND GRADER, UNCLE DAN'S
REPORT CARD KANSAS PILOT PROGRAM

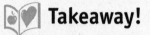 Takeaway!

- Stick around during bath time. Part of the routine can be a parent staying in the bathroom during the bath. Children will look forward to spending time together. Use bath time as a social ritual, by discussing the day's events while bathing your little ones. As children grow into the modest stage of development and no longer want parents to be in the room during bath time, they will have gotten into the bath routine and be more likely to take personal responsibility for their good grooming.

Care of Clothing

Ornamental articles of dress cause most regret when they are lost or torn. It is not so much the fear of punishment as the idea to do without the thing they like or are proud of that causes them worry. Miss Rusling thinks her results show that accidents to children's clothing are not always due to natural depravity, because so many feel sad at their loss. That boys are as vain about clothes as girls. That little boys worry most when their hats are temporarily mislaid, but that girls seem more attached to mittens and coats.

—STUDY BY MISS LILLIAN A. RUSLING IN *THE PEDAGOGICAL SEMINARY*, VOL. XII, 1905, EDITED BY G. STANLEY HALL

Why "Care of Clothing" Mattered Then

When we think about our dapperly dressed Dan, it's hard to believe he only received a mark of "Good" from his parents in this subject. Did they set the bar high to impress upon him the importance of Care of Clothing? Whatever the case, it worked. Well into his nineties, his large closet was full of suits, ties, suspenders, handkerchiefs, and shoes, all freshly cleaned, neatly hung, folded, or polished.

Care of clothing was all about being responsible and thrifty, both signs of people of good character. Being well dressed required stretching the family budget, but it was worth it to send a neatly dressed child out of the home to represent "good breeding." Pants and socks that showed proper repair reflected on a mother's sewing ability, too.

In 1914, clothing was either handmade or was expensive if bought in local stores, so parents hoped children only outgrew, rather than wore out, clothing so it could be passed down to younger siblings. It was necessary to patch tears and holes as well as to darn holes in socks, so that they could be worn as long as possible.

Shoes in 1914 were made of leather and were the most expensive articles of clothing. To make shoes last, they were brushed and polished with wax to preserve the surface of the leather. When the soles of shoes wore out, a piece of cardboard might be inserted inside to cover the hole to keep the bottom of the sock from being exposed through the hole. Eventually new soles could be put on the shoes by the shoemaker, so the shoes could last even longer. Brushing and polishing shoes before bed became a part of the daily ritual of clothing care.

Why "Care of Clothing" Matters Today

Teaching a child to care for his clothing from an early age is one daily activity that can help him learn responsibility for his belongings and the importance of personal appearance. Picking things up from the floor of his room, hanging his coat up when coming into the house, and protecting clothes from spills when eating or doing art projects, for example, create a habit of self-respect that is important to build from a child's earliest years forward. When a child has a closet of neat and tidy clothes, he is more likely to feel proud of how he looks and confident in his appearance.

Today, even preschoolers get powerful media messages about what they should be "wearing" and are often influenced by peer pressure to wear "what's cool." So for many families, it is fashion, as much as finances, that dictates what is worn by children. Regardless of the amount of clothing a family can afford or the price tag of each item, caring for clothes is a timeless way for parents to teach a child to value his possessions and not give in to peer pressure to quit wearing clothes that are no longer in style.

Even in the name of teaching children responsibility, getting children interested in taking care of their clothing is difficult. Other things take priority: sports, video games, music lessons, social media, schoolwork, smart phones, and TV. One of the more frequently cited conflicts between parents and children is about the clothing scattered on the floor of their room. Children see no sense in putting away things they are going to wear again soon anyway! Immediate reward verses long-term gain? The former wins out today in children's minds!

HOW TO TEACH A CHILD TO CARE FOR CLOTHING

⊜ **Be an Uncle Dan.** When children see you taking care of your clothing and talking to them about what you are doing and why you are doing it, they are more likely to consider care of clothing as something important to do. Children learn most from what they see adults doing.

⊜ **Make clothing rules.** Children respond better to rules rather than just being told what to do. Rules are viewed as belonging to the world rather than just something parents say. Say, "The rule is, underwear and socks must be put away in this drawer."

⊜ **Practice, practice, practice.** Practicing putting clothing away properly will make the behavior more likely to stick around. Say, "The rule is, dirty clothes go in the laundry basket. Now, let's practice putting these things you left on the floor in the hamper. We'll do it five times."

⊜ **Praise, praise, praise.** Children are more likely to follow the clothing rules when you praise them for following them. You can even praise what's about to happen: "I see you are about to put that dirty shirt in the laundry basket. That's so helpful to me."

⊜ **When you have . . . then you may.** Make taking care of clothing mandatory before children are allowed to play, watch TV, get online, text, tweet, or do any other fun activity. "When you have put away your clothes, then you may go over to El-len's house."

————

My children actually got excited about doing a task that would allow them to put a mark on their card, even putting their clothes away.

—PARENT OF A FIRST GRADER, UNCLE DAN'S
REPORT CARD KANSAS PILOT PROGRAM

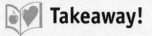 **Takeaway!**

- The value of caring for personal belongings is a long-term lesson. Since children are concerned with immediate reward, they need to be taught that caring for their clothes and other personal belongings is one of their responsibilities.

HABIT ELEVEN

Sleeping, Windows Open

The custom of opening windows in our bedrooms at night is grad-ually gaining a foothold. It has been positively established that night air does not differ from day air, except that it is freer from dust and smoke; otherwise it is exactly the same thing, and as some sanitarians have put it, "the only night air that is danger-ous is last night's—open the windows and let it out. There is no occasion for any one being afraid of a draft if they are warmly covered up on their beds at night."

—A REPORT FROM THE INDIANA STATE BOARD OF HEALTH,
PUBLISHED IN THE KANSAS DEPARTMENT OF HEALTH BULLETIN,
NO. 10, OCTOBER 1913

Why "Sleeping, Windows Open" Mattered Then

Of all the habits on Uncle Dan's report card, this one leaves everyone puzzled. Why was it so important to sleep with "win-dows open"? It's also the habit for which Dan received the greatest variation of marks: "G, G, E, M, G." Perhaps the temperatures dropped sharply during the week Dan received his M!

It was strongly believed that dusty air was a major cause of sickness in children. In *Care and Feeding of Children*, Dr. Holt devotes an entire chapter to "Airing":

> Airing in the room may be begun, even in cold weather, when the child is one month old, at first for only fifteen minutes at a time. This period may be gradually lengthened by ten or fifteen minutes each day until it is four or five hours. This airing may be continued in almost all kinds of weather.

Fresh air was considered a combatant to tuberculosis and anemia. "Fresh air" schools and open-air playgrounds for children were promoted, in part according to *Advances in Child Development and Behavior*, "driven by public health concerns and in part by a rural nostalgia." Many people of the time held "a faith in fresh air that was strong."

In 1901, the *Oral Lesson Book in Hygiene for Primary Teachers* encouraged teachers to ask:

> Where besides in our schoolrooms should we be careful to have pure air? Explain that we need plenty of pure air in the rooms we live in at home and in the rooms where we sleep.

What about the problem of houseflies? Flies were considered a serious matter and carriers of all kinds of disease. Lots of ads in the *Kansas City Kansan* promoted window screens like this one:

BUY YOUR SCREEN FROM US
Protect Yourself from the Filthy Housefly

The June 30, 1914, Kansas State Board of Health Bulletin shared an idea to rid a community of flies. Hutchinson, Kansas, held an "All-Summer Fly Crusade," inviting children to bring their dead flies to the porch of the Convention Hall on Monday mornings. "We will pay Two Silver Dollars to the boy or girl bringing the most dead flies, and One Silver Dollar to the boy or girl bringing the next largest quantity of Dead Flies." Now that's a clever combination of getting marks on many entries of the Home Report at one time: Hours Worked, Money Earned, Helping Mother, and Helping Father!

Why "Sleeping, Windows Open" Matters Today

Helping children get a healthy amount of sleep matters today, whether the windows are open or not! Parents need to be focusing their attention on *how much* sleep their child is getting in order for him to be at his best. It is well known that children need sufficient sleep, nutritious food, and exercise to help their brains work as well as they can. Today, many children don't get enough sleep; and sleep deprivation makes them sleepy, dopey, and grumpy in school during the day, not a good condition for learning.

Because houses today are heated and air-conditioned, most people don't want to open their windows. In addition, many would have to contend with air pollution, pollen, and noxious odors, making sleeping with the windows open uncomfortable. The health benefits of night air that convinced people to sleep with windows open a century ago were exaggerated, and the fad eventually faded; so today people prefer and pay dearly for heated or cooled, filtered air to breathe in bed at night.

HOW TO TEACH YOUR CHILD TO GET A HEALTHY AMOUNT OF SLEEP

- **Be an Uncle Dan.** Children learn much of their behavior from watching the adults in their lives, so you need to show children by your own behavior how important it is to get adequate exercise, fresh air, and enough sleep.

- **Decide on an appropriate bedtime for your child.** Five-year-old children need about eleven hours of sleep in a twenty-four-hour period, and eight-year-old children need ten hours of sleep. By the time your child is fourteen, he'll still need nine and a half hours of sleep each night.

- **Use a bedtime routine that allows your child to calm herself and relax before bed.** Reading to her for a few minutes before bedtime is a good quiet activity.

⊜ **Use a timer to control your child's bedtime routine.** Getting ready for bed before the timer rings can be a fun game that earns your child reading time.

———

Uncle Dan's Report Card is the only tool that worked to get kindergartners to school on time.

—PRINCIPAL OF AN ELEMENTARY SCHOOL, UNCLE DAN'S REPORT CARD KANSAS PILOT PROGRAM

Takeaway!

- Ensuring adequate sleep each night is important to promote your child's school success. Even losing an hour's sleep each night will have a noticeable effect on your child's performance. Research has demonstrated that sleep deficiency may harm brain development in young children and can contribute to school problems, such as attention deficit/hyperactivity disorder.

HABIT TWELVE

Manners

If one would learn something of the home from which a child comes, all that is necessary is to watch him at play and listen to him. If he habitually says "please," and "thank you," if he refrains from interrupting, if he does not squabble and contradict, if he is unselfish, it is easy to see he come from a family where good breeding reigns.

—*THE MOTHERS' BOOK: SUGGESTIONS REGARDING THE MENTAL AND MORAL DEVELOPMENT OF CHILDREN,* BY CAROLINE BENEDICT BURRELL, 1909

Why "Manners" Mattered Then

Manners were the social clothing people wore that helped them fit into the highest level of society they wanted to belong to. Their "worthiness" and their manners were synonymous: "Joe must be an important person, because he uses good manners."

In the section of the Twenty-Fifth Annual Report of the Board of Education of the City of Kansas City, Kansas, June 30, 1911, titled, "Teaching of Manners," Ethel Anderson, the principal of Armstrong School, wrote:

There is so much to be gained through the exercise of good manners that it is amazing that greater attention is not paid to training the young in this very important branch of education. Character is formed by training, rather than by teaching. A teacher cannot lecture a child into good manners, nor change the habits of any kind by the longest speech. Habits are only a repetition of doing, and it is in these doings that training consists.

School life affords many opportunities for instruction in moral and ethical training. No longer are these lessons crowded into a corner and given the "odds and ends" of school time. They have been assigned a regular place in the weekly program and receive their due share of attention. The first practice of manners should begin at home. Good manners in the household are like oil upon complicated machinery, they are more important than anything else in their strong influence upon character. The result of refined manners in early life shows itself in all that a man or woman becomes.

Why "Manners" Matters Today

The practice of good manners enables us to reconnect with people around us and society as a whole through the development of empathy, simply by considering the age-old adage to "treat others as we would like to be treated."

Children today have become increasingly isolated to the point of communicating with the world outside themselves through email, texts, and tweets. Although Facebook and other social media help them stay connected to others, in reality, they often exchange words with "friends" they don't really know and may never meet in person.

When face-to-face contact is missing, the need and opportunities to practice good manners fade away. If someone is hurt by words or behavior, we usually don't see it—literally—in our most pervasive forms of expression of today, including voicemails, texts, and email messages. Empathy—the ability to identify with another person's feelings—suffers thanks to the reliance on electronic communication and the increasingly self-centered focus of today's society. When humans lived in caves, empathy was important, as the members of a group needed to be able to rely on each other for survival. A human without empathy would be thrown out of the group and eaten by saber-toothed tigers! But as we have become more isolated and materialistic, this community-centered focus has become less important. When people lust after things, they have less time for people. Getting more things leads to the dog-eat-dog culture we see today. It isn't possible to have empathy for an opponent when winning is the only goal. Social relationships suffer without empathy, which leads to more isolation.

Communicating through words alone only conveys about 7 percent of the meaning of the communication because facial expression, body language, and history make up the rest. Meeting people face-to-face brings completeness to social interaction and allows the communication of feelings. Humans, after all, are actually *feeling* animals who think, so taking feelings out of social interaction is like walking with one leg. The constant use of electronics to communicate is handicapping people to such an extent that their ability to feel anything except anger and rage is blunted.

HOW TO TEACH A CHILD MANNERS

✏ **Decide what manners are good for your family.** The Child Development Institute, an online resource for parents, suggests focusing on manners in five areas: home manners, telephone manners, table manners, guest manners, and street manners.

✏ **Make a list.** Having manners posted prominently serves as a reminder to all of what is expected of them. For preschoolers and elementary-age children, model, reinforce, and practice behaviors on the list, such as:

- How and when to use *please, thank you, you're welcome, excuse me, may I*, and *I'm sorry*.
- Proper use of napkins (in laps).
- Proper sitting (not slouching) at dinner.
- Use of appropriate language that excludes profanity and popular phrases that discount others and demonstrate disrespect, such as "shut up," "whatever," and "good luck with that."

• No texting or answering a cell phone at meals or during a conversation.

• Making eye contact when being spoken to and shaking hands when meeting someone, saying, "Nice to meet you" when introduced.

✏ **Be an Uncle Dan.** Model good manners for children, so they will see you doing what you expect of them. Describe your manners to make sure your children know what manners you are demonstrating. Say, for example, "You see, I used good manners by knocking on your door before coming in. That respects your privacy."

✏ **Talk to your children.** Explain good manners by saying, "Good manners are a way to show consideration and respect for others and to help people respect who you are and want to be around you. They help others feel good when they're with you."

✏ **Praise, praise, praise.** Describe the good manners you are seeing your children using and show your approval. Say, for example, "You waited until I stopped talking before you talked. That's showing good manners."

✏ **Be positive.** Pointing out the behavior you want is a much better way to motivate than nagging. We all like positives rather than negatives, so use positive reactions whenever you can. Children want your approval, so give it to them when you see them doing what you like.

⊟ **Practice becomes habit.** Only talking about behavior doesn't teach how to do the behavior. Having practice sessions converts talk into behavior and helps it stick around. Say, for example, "Let's practice using our napkins tonight," or "I know it's hard to remember to chew with your mouth closed, so let's practice."

I've already seen a positive change in my children's habits and manners in just six weeks.

—PARENT OF A KINDERGARTNER, UNCLE DAN'S
REPORT CARD KANSAS PILOT PROGRAM

 ## Takeaways!

- The preschool years are an apprenticeship for going to school. Learning good manners during this period ensures greater success in school.

- Researcher Albert Mehrabian suggests that only 7 percent of communication rests in the words used. The remainder lies in body language, context, facial expression, and the experiences each person brings to the interaction.

- The University of Virginia researcher Jonathan Haidt has shown that all children come into the world with empathy hardwired in them. It's up to the adults in the child's world to bring that empathy out, so the child can better understand others and use her imagination to express what she is feeling.

- Empathy is the key to emotional intelligence, which leads to greater chances for success in the workplace, according to Daniel Goleman, author of *Emotional Intelligence* and *Social Intelligence*.

- Manners help us all work and play well with others. Using good manners in school keeps children in good standing with teachers.

- Good manners are a social lubricant. Shy children with good manners can rely on their manners to get them through uncomfortable social situations and build confidence.

- Manners lead to empathy and help keep us connected to others. Imagining the feelings of others keeps us from exploiting them.

- The Child Development Institute lists the three C's of manners: custom, consideration, and common sense. One more needs to be added—consistency.

- Table manners can only be taught by having dinner together as a family. Sandra Hofferth and John Sandberg, of the University of Michigan, have found that children who have meals with their families excel more in school, have better behavior, get along better with peers, and have higher self-confidence.

Helping Father

Here children do not receive everything as a gift; according to the measure of their power they must share in the work of the home; they learn to take account of their parents, of servants, and one another.

—*CENTURY OF THE CHILD*, BY ELLEN KEY, 1909

Why "Helping Father" Mattered Then

In 1914, children's help was needed to keep the family going, whether that family lived in a city or on a farm. Work was thought to build character and to be a part of the educational mission. Now we know when Uncle Dan developed his legendary work ethic. After all, this was a man who worked long days and for a long time. He retired from his law practice at the age of ninety!

A study of a West Side neighborhood in New York City in 1914 reported, "Not only will a boy not go far afield for his games, but he cannot. He is often at home after school hours to run errands and make himself generally useful."

Urban houses offered chances for doing many chores that were in the father's domain. In winter, the coal furnace had to be stoked and the ash removed and spread in the alley behind the house. Bringing coal for the kitchen stove and hauling out the ashes was a year-round job many boys were assigned. Bringing buckets of water from the kitchen and putting them in a boiler to heat for washday were other duties often reserved for the males of the family.

For Dan, after school may have meant a stop at the furniture store that his father owned, where he could run errands, deliver goods, wait on customers, sweep the store, stock shelves, move boxes in the storeroom, and do any number of small chores. Or with Adolph having little time for home chores, Dan could pitch in to keep the house and the yard in tip-top condition. The local newspaper during this time was filled with promotions by the city urging the citizens to show pride in their city by cleaning up their yards, painting their fences, and cleaning their sidewalks.

Dan and his siblings could also help their father by planting and tending the family garden. Dan could show off the skills he learned working at the school garden. The 1916 *Kansas City Kansan* reported that 451 boys and girls worked in the school plots and gardens, and 2,000 gardens were planned for the next year!

Why "Helping Father" Matters Today

Instead of children helping their father or mother, often the reverse is true today. Parents end up helping their children fill their free time by organizing games and lessons, and buying toys and electronics that keep the children busy. Many children don't see their fathers during the week because their schedules don't intersect.

Parenting roles have changed in this twenty-first century with more time spent out of the home. In a series of long-term studies conducted by the UCLA Center on Everyday Lives of Families, several trends were noted:

- Because of parents' work schedules and children's lesson and sports schedules, parents and children live virtually apart at least five days a week and reunite for a few hours at night. At least one parent is likely to be up and gone before the children awake, so breakfast together as a family is impossible.

- In fact, as a result of the fast pace and overscheduling, family life has become like a small business that requisitions supplies and lives in disorganized clutter.

- Twenty percent of today's two-year-olds have TVs in their bedrooms and, therefore, spend time isolated from the rest of the family.

HOW TO TEACH A CHILD TO HELP FATHER

- **Make a list of chores that would help Father.** (Note: If chores are shared equally by the mother and the father, then explain to your children that these jobs are not gender specific.) It's much easier to keep track of chores when they are listed. See if you can find age-appropriate things children can do, such as vacuuming out the car, bringing in the newspaper, sorting the mail, finding the remote, programming the TV, and trouble-shooting the computer.

- **Reward helpfulness.** We all prefer to work for things rather than work to avoid punishment, so give privileges for children's helpfulness.

- **When you have . . . then you may.** This basic contract simply offers all privileges in exchange for chore completion. Say, for example, "When you have finished painting the fence, then you may go outside and play."

- **Praise, praise, praise.** All dads need to keep their eye out for their child's helpfulness. Describe the helpful behavior, and tell the child how much the behavior is appreciated.

Now I'm able to let my children feel more responsible for their own daily activities.

—PARENT OF A SECOND GRADER, UNCLE DAN'S
REPORT CARD KANSAS PILOT PROGRAM

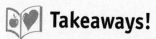 **Takeaways!**

- Society is moving from being "child-centered" to "child-dominated," with children dictating the family's schedule of activities, which works against learning to be helpful.

- Family relationships have to be scheduled and are often outsourced to teachers and coaches. The "face time" spent together doing tasks builds more than the skill of helpfulness. It also cements the relationship between a father and his child.

Helping Mother

It is one of the greatest mistakes that a mother can make, to excuse her children from helping her in her daily tasks; nothing makes them grow up so hard, so bent on pleasure, as to let them have all the easy times while their mother takes the burdens on her own shoulders and spares them.

—THE MOTHERS' BOOK: SUGGESTIONS REGARDING THE MENTAL AND MORAL DEVELOPMENT OF CHILDREN, BY CAROLINE BENEDICT BURRELL, 1909

Why "Helping Mother" Mattered Then

Helping Mother did not always mean home chores. For some families, helping mother meant industrial homework, factory work done at home, mostly by mothers with their young children. According to *Pricing the Priceless Child*, this "usually involved immigrant families or other unskilled low-paid groups living in the tenement districts of large cities. Industrial homework included a wide range of activities, chiefly finishing men's clothing, embroidering, making artificial flowers, and stringing tags. Children helped with the simpler tasks and often delivered the work from home to the factory."

In "Training the Girl to Help in the Home," a 1909 bulletin, William McKeever's interviews with mothers included tips like this one:

> Home training should be begun early, from three to seven years. Just as soon as my girls became interested in dolls and toy dishes, I tried to take advantage of this fact in their training . . . while the care of these playthings was a matter of amusement to them, I saw at the same time that they were learning something. It was not a very difficult matter to lead them from the play to the work of the same nature.

But it was unlikely that Dan and his brother and sisters let their mother do any work on May 10, 1914 . . . the first Mother's Day! President Woodrow Wilson made it official: Mother's Day would be a national holiday held each year on the second Sunday in May. He stated that mothers were "the greatest source of the country's strength and inspiration." He ordered the U.S. flag displayed on all public buildings to honor mothers.

Why "Helping Mother" Matters Today

While children are in after-school care, both parents may be winding down their long hours at work outside the home. When all arrive home, the rush is on to eat dinner, do homework, brush teeth, and get into bed at a reasonable time. Weekends devoted to sports and lessons leave little downtime to take care of the myriad chores that need to be done. As the old saying goes, "The hurrier I go the behinder I get!"

Is it possible or even desirable to try to recapture the concept of being helpful to Mother today by doing the daily chores that she does around the house, including cooking, cleaning, and gardening? What would children learn from such an exercise? With all the labor-saving machines at a mother's disposal today, what's left to do?

First, let's look at overindulged children, who have too many things, too much help, and too few requirements at home. They have an exaggerated sense of their own self-worth, and feel entitled to have all these things for which they've never had to work. As a result, these children are often depressed because they feel empty of purpose. At school, they are faced with hard work, when they would rather be at home, where they can play. They are connected to the world through their phones and computers, so they can escape from the drudgery of responsibilities in seconds.

This sounds as if it is a recipe for creating a generation of children who are lazy and unmotivated. And it is. But it gets worse. Parents today are avoiding assigning chores to children to help maintain order at home. They don't want to fight with their children about getting them done. It is simply much easier to do the work and avoid the hassle. If chores are assigned, many children aren't held to a standard of excellence and, without any accountability, are often excused from the poorly done chore, which is redone by a parent.

Having chores to complete on a daily basis has been found to be the best antidote for the overindulged syndrome. Chores offer purpose, build skills, and give satisfaction when completed well. In short, chores build character, something that appeared to be well known in 1914.

HOW TO TEACH A CHILD TO HELP MOTHER

- **Assign chores.** Talk with your children about these jobs being gender-free. They may not necessarily be "mother's jobs" but those that Mom has taken responsibility for doing around the house. Even preschool children can accomplish chores, such as picking up toys, putting books back on the shelf, putting clean clothes in a drawer, and other simple tasks. For older children, cleaning, vacuuming, setting the table, clearing the table, filling and emptying the dishwasher, and helping prepare meals are good examples.

- **Be an Uncle Dan.** Show children how to do the jobs you've assigned. Children learn better from demonstration than from lecture. Spare the words and show the child.

- **Praise, praise, praise.** When a chore is complete, point out the parts that have been done correctly and then say that the chore will be complete when that part that wasn't done well is finished. We all thrive on praise, so use it liberally.

✎ **Make lists.** Children often prefer a list of things to do rather than being told what to do. Lists also reduce your own involvement because you can check the completion all at once instead of after assigning each task. In the business world, using lists of goals is called "management by objectives."

✎ **Make chore completion the ticket to freedom.** Grandma had a rule that said, "When you have finished what you have to do, then you may do what you want to do." Work first, play after. You may have to keep your child's cell phone while her chores are being done; then return it upon successful completion of the job.

✎ **Tell your children how helpful they are being.** When you say, "I appreciate your help so much," you encourage your children to think of the impact they have on the greater good, a good thing for them to keep in mind in order to be successful in relationships at school and in work throughout life.

It fits into our state standards for social studies, including being a good citizen.

—ELEMENTARY SCHOOL TEACHER, UNCLE DAN'S
REPORT CARD KANSAS PILOT PROGRAM

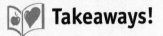 **Takeaways!**

- Share stories with your child about chores you did as a child.

- Point out the chores that are your personal responsibility and those that are hers.

- Let your child check off the chore on his chore list when he's done, to recognize that he has taken care of his personal responsibilities.

- Preschoolers love to be helpful, so rewarding their help-fulness with your praise reinforces that positive be-havior and begins the habit of working for the greater good.

- Children who help around the house gain a sense of pur-pose and self-worth. Therefore, they are less prone to depression, the common cold of mental health.

Morning Duties

As child work shifted from instrumental to instructional, special consideration was given to domestic chores. When an article appearing in *Home Progress* advised parents, "Let your children work," the work referred to "some little household task," not too difficult of course, "for their tender bodies." . . . House chores were therefore not intended to be "real" work, but lessons in helpfulness, order, and unselfishness.

—*PRICING THE PRICELESS CHILD: THE CHANGING SOCIAL VALUE OF CHILDREN,*
BY VIVIANA A. ZELIZER, 1985

Why "Morning Duties" Mattered Then

Not only were morning duties necessary for the day to get started smoothly with the help of each family member, but they also provided training for developing responsibility and a good work ethic.

In the June 1919 edition of *Primary Education*, Eliza Emery shares a system for teaching duties from the National Tuberculosis Association called "A Record of Health Chores." Here duties are used to help form healthy habits, such as washing hands, brushing teeth, keeping dirty things out of one's mouth, etc. As it suggests, "If your boy or girl does the following chores or duties faithfully for one week he will be taught a valuable lesson; if he keeps them up strictly for two or more weeks he will likely form health habits for life."

In *Century of the Child*, Ellen Key recommended that parents let the child "help himself":

What is required, above all, for the children of the present day, is to be assigned again real home occupations, tasks they must do conscientiously, habits of work arranged for weekdays and holidays without oversight, in every case where the child can help himself. Instead of the modern school child having a mother and servants about him to get him ready for school and to help him to remember things, he should have time every day before school to arrange his room and brush his clothes, and there should be no effort to make him remember what is connected with the school. The home and the school should combine together systematically to let the child suffer for the results of his own negligence.

Why "Morning Duties" Matters Today

One fear remains unchanged from 1914: parents' concern that children have become reluctant participants in the family, as parents have become more and more entrenched in their own jobs, and more helpful to their children rather than the reverse. What can be done so that children are not considered a "burden"? A parent today struggles to get them up, fed, dressed, and off to school or day care so they can get to their jobs. Many a parent has lamented the chaos every morning of getting children moving, and talks about the crying and screaming that accompanies morning routines. Instead of feeling like a contributing member of the family, children sense their fifth-wheel status. In order to gain recognition in the family, children today often create conflict, which is guaranteed to get parents to react. Cooperation with the family agenda carries no such guarantee.

Key's message to early-twentieth-century mothers is still relevant to early-twenty-first-century mothers:

> Just the reverse of this system rules today. Mothers learn their children's lessons, invent plays for them, ready their story books to them, arrange their rooms after them, pick up what they have let fall, put in order the things they have left in confusion, and in this and in other ways, by protective pampering and attention, their desire for work, their endurance, the gifts of invention and imagination, qualities proper to the child, become weak and passive.
>
> They are trained to be always receptive instead of giving something in return. Then people are surprised at a youthful generation, selfish and unrestrained,

pressing forward shamelessly on all occasions before their elders, crudely unresponsive in respect of those attentions, which in earlier generations were a beautiful custom among the young.

HOW TO TEACH A CHILD MORNING DUTIES

- **Establish a routine.** Children thrive on routine. Because they are relatively new to the world, they don't always know what to expect, and routine allows them to anticipate what's going to happen next.

- **Practice, practice, practice.** Before expecting children to do what you want every morning, walk through the routine several times in the evening, so the routine demonstrates the behaviors you want.

- **Use a timer.** Children love to race, so let them race the clock getting dressed, brushing teeth, cleaning up after breakfast, and completing other morning chores. A kitchen timer is helpful, and you can simply say, "Let's see if you can beat the timer doing . . ."

- **Praise, praise, praise.** Children need praise for what they do, as well as what they are about to do. "I see you are thinking about putting your bowl in the dishwasher. That's so helpful to me."

✏ **When you have . . . then you may.** This basic contract can help motivate children in morning chores. When chores are done, the child may read, play, or do something else enjoyable. Work first, play after.

I got great responses from the families in my class. I even had one family ask for extras to use with their younger children. I'm excited that we have gotten such a good response from the staff and families in our school community.

—ELEMENTARY SCHOOL TEACHER, UNCLE DAN'S
REPORT CARD KANSAS PILOT PROGRAM

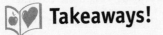 # Takeaways!

- Help your child devise a system of organizing what she takes to school, including books, lunch, and notes, as her primary morning duty during the school year.

- Establish a routine at home, so notes from home will be delivered to school each morning.

- Help your child be prepared for the morning duties of getting ready for camp, school, practices, or other activities by talking through the next day's schedule the night before.

Evening Duties

In teaching the child to assume responsibility, the mother will, of course, assign to each those duties that are best suited to his or her capacity. Each child should have a special routine of duties; for while it will at first seem rather difficult to the mother to explain over and over how each task is to be performed, she will in time receive the reward of her perseverance. The duties should be light and simple at the start and increase in number and importance as the child gains in age and in experience.

—*CHILD LIFE, PHYSICAL AND MENTAL DEVELOPMENT,*
METROPOLITAN PAMPHLET SERIES, 1895

Why "Evening Duties" Mattered Then

The 72-page pamphlet *Child Life, Physical and Mental Development* stated that by assigning evening duties, such as filling water pitchers, hanging up fresh towels, seeing that the soap and matches are in their "proper places," dusting the furniture, pulling out basting threads, and turning down the bed covers at night, "the little workers soon acquire the habit of responsibility."

Just as with the morning duties, evening duties were also

important to keep the family going while it was still light. Candles, kerosene, gas, and electricity were costly, so utilizing daylight was important. After homework, firewood might be needed, the work of preparing supper started, laundry was folded and put away, water pumped and carried to the kitchen.

For children whose parents had a business, work in the shop was a part of evening duties. Sweeping the shop, putting away goods, making deliveries, waiting on customers, all would be a part of evening duties. Older children took care of younger children by helping with feeding, getting them ready for bed, helping pick up toys, and completing other tasks that freed parents to do different things. In 1914, home was a workplace, and in comparison, school was not.

Why "Evening Duties" Matters Today

Many children spend their evening being transported from one practice or lesson to another. (See Habit 7, "Evenings at Home," page 69.) Homework is done in transit, and dinner is fast food eaten from a bag. But not being home every evening is no excuse for parents to ignore assigning their child evening duties. Opportunities for a child to get in the habit of being helpful and to develop a good work ethic are more plentiful than ever. The difference is that today these duties may or may not always be done at home: a child may be helpful by getting his musical instruments or soccer gear into the trunk of the car, feeding the younger children at a restaurant, picking out items at the grocery store, or baby-sitting her sibling while Mom is at her evening job, for example.

Evening is also an important time of day for parents to teach children to be responsible for completing their school homework assignments. The good news is that with all of these evening duties for today's busy children, there is little time for them to spend aimless hours watching DVDs, texting their friends, and talking on the phone. Perhaps this is the most important reason that evening duties matter today!

HOW TO TEACH A CHILD EVENING DUTIES

- **Make a checklist.** Children prefer following a list of duties to being told what to do, so give each child a list of things you would like him to do in the evening.

- **Set a time limit.** Children need to know that they have a deadline to meet, so they learn timeliness. Make the deadline meaningful. For example, carrying out the trash the day after the scheduled pickup falls short of the goal, so getting it out on time needs to be included on the list.

- **Praise, praise, praise.** We are all motivated by praise, so praise the effort being made even before completion of the task to maintain positive momentum.

- **When you have . . . then you may.** Work before play includes keeping cell phones out of your child's hands until tasks are complete. This rule includes homework, which fades in quality with frequent interruptions to send and receive texts.

⮫ **Make rules about screen time.** Children need to practice being "in the moment" with other humans. Putting restrictions on screen time, including TV, computer, and cell phones, will give your child experience in being free and unplugged. The constant adrenaline of always being "on" and accessible while doing something else is addictive. Research is proving that an excessive amount of screen time is changing children's brain patterns, and causing them to have difficulty focusing and paying attention.

———

The Report Card motivated my kids to practice these habits. They got excited about putting another sticker on their Report Card.

—PARENT OF A PRESCHOOLER, UNCLE DAN'S
REPORT CARD KANSAS PILOT PROGRAM

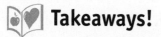 **Takeaways!**

- A University of Michigan study found that more mealtime at home was the single strongest predictor of better achievement scores and fewer behavior problems.

- Child development researchers found that children's social skills atrophy when children watch TV instead of playing.

- Research has found that watching several hours of TV each day reduces children's reading skills by addicting them to fast-paced, emotionally charged images rather than creating images in their minds based on words they're reading.

- A national study has concluded that four-year-olds watching the daily average of 3.5 hours of television were 25 percent more likely to become bullies.

- A school night filled with the fun of playing video games or watching television makes the prospect of sitting in school more difficult, owing to the decrease in learning readiness.

- Researchers found that children who have chores to do learn to develop realistic expectations for themselves, have greater self-confidence, and develop good work skills.

- The American Academy of Pediatrics recommends, "Pediatricians should urge parents to avoid television viewing for children under the age of two years. Although certain television programs may be promoted to this age group, research on early brain development shows that babies and toddlers have a critical need for direct interactions with parents and other significant caregivers (e.g., child care providers) for healthy brain growth and the development of appropriate social, emotional, and cognitive skills. Therefore, exposing such young children to television programs should be discouraged."

HABIT SEVENTEEN

Obedience and Promptness

Often a child in the home is regarded as rebellious when it is merely trying to adjust its reason to the demands made by the parent. It argues, objects, finds fault and is difficult to manage, and parents do not understand that the difficulty lies in the fact that the child has an unusually well-developed reasoning faculty and probably a vigorous body as well. Such a child needs training, not punishment.

—"MANAGING THE CHILD," *KANSAS CITY KANSAN*, APRIL 20, 1916

Why "Obedience and Promptness" Mattered Then

Why were obedience and promptness held in such high regard back in Uncle Dan's day? Because these behaviors were considered building blocks in the making of responsible, reliable citizens. It was also understood that a system of authority is needed to live together in a community. The culture of 1914 held responsible citizenship to be paramount in building a functioning society. All people were thought to be a part of a living social organism, and if each played his part, all would benefit.

In school, following the rules ensured that children would

learn and achieve. In the workplace, following the rules led to work completion and a successful company. Having a framework of rules in the culture of 1914 made life predictable. People knew what to expect from each other and felt comfortable in that culture. *The Mothers' Book* said it this way:

> Obedience is the first principle of training in social life; and it must be insisted upon in children by parents, not because they are their parents, or have any inborn authority over them personally—for there is no such thing—but because it is for the child's good and for the safety of society. The parents having added a prospective citizen to the state become responsible that, so far as they can effect it, he shall become a law-abiding one.
>
> Punctuality is another of the lessons which children must learn. When sent upon errands they should be forbidden to loiter along the way. They should be taught that time is a treasure which, once lost, can never be recovered.

When it came to matters of obedience in the school, punctuality was singled out. In the 1911 Kansas City School Board Report section titled "Regularity and Punctuality," Margaret Cathcart, the principal of Stanley School, wrote:

> It seems to me that regularity and punctuality are two essentials requisite to the success of any undertaking,

no matter if it be the management of the home, the school, or life in the business or social world.

Teachers and pupils should not think they have done their whole duty in this respect by being in school on time and at all sessions; they should also manifest a promptness in meeting every requirement of the day.

Tillie did her part at home to reinforce obedience and punctuality. She awarded Dan with E's and G's on his Home Report!

Why "Obedience and Promptness" Matters Today

Obedience and *promptness* are words that bring back not only a sense of nostalgia, but also the necessity of returning civility to our children's lives at home and school. Being subservient to authority, required in obedience, is seen as a loss of freedom today. As a result, in the name of freedom, rules have been tossed aside and dismissed as unnecessary. And life without rules has become more unpredictable. This lack of predictability has led to fear, anxiety, and a need for structure in children's lives.

The current "plugged in" culture demands immediacy in communication but not in task completion. Following rules takes a backseat to being connected. The only rules that are important are those dictated by phone services, online services, and social networking services.

Just as in 1914, children today who have learned to follow

rules and to fulfill obligations on time are more successful in school. They forge a social contract with their parents and teachers that says they will live up to their obligations and will not be distracted. They will do what they have to do before they do what they want to do. They will have the skills needed to be successful in life.

However, blind obedience, that willingness to follow the dictates of an authority figure, has its dangers, as was pointed out by Stanley Milgram in the research he conducted in 1963 at Yale University. He found that ordinary people can be easily made to be obedient to the extent that they will significantly harm another person. These people found it more important to be obedient to the authority figure than to save another person severe pain. Milgram's research makes it imperative for authority figures to demand obedience in only the most socially acceptable areas of children's lives, those areas that benefit society rather than bring harm.

HOW TO TEACH A CHILD OBEDIENCE AND PROMPTNESS TODAY

⊜ **Decide what rules would be good for your family**. We all need rules in our lives to guide us, and teaching children to follow rules is the road to obedience. Rules should be positive and tell children what to do, rather than what not to do. (See "The Do's and Don'ts of Using Uncle Dan's Report Card," page 27.)

✏ **Make a list of family rules.** When rules are on a list, they are easier to enforce; lists reduce arguments about the rule, and children are reminded of the rules when they see the list.

✏ **Be an Uncle Dan.** Parents have to model obedience and promptness by following the family rules and traffic laws. Striving always to be on time shows children that promptness counts.

✏ **Praise, praise, praise.** When your children follow the rules and show up on time, lavish praise by describing what they did and telling them how much you appreciate their effort.

✏ **Practice makes habit.** When a rule is violated, a consequence can be having your child practice the rule several times before being allowed to do what he wants to do. For example, if you have a rule that coats must be hung in the hall closet and the rule is violated, then the child is required to put the coat on, take it off, and hang it up five times.

✏ **Obligations before fun.** When children have done what they have to do, such as chores, homework, and writing a letter to Grandma, then they may do what they want to do, within the house rules. TV, video games, cell phones, iPods, and other games may be used after obligations are met.

✏ **Teach appropriate verbal response to requests.** When asked to do something appropriate, the polite response is "Okay" or "Yes, I'll do it," instead of saying, "Whatever" or "Good luck with that!" for example. Teaching this helps encourage manners, as well as obedience.

- **Set a time limit for completion.** Say, for example, "Homework must be done before dinner. Rooms must be picked up before bed."

- **Always give directions that tell your child what you want him to do, rather than what you don't want him to do.** For example, say, "Please ask an adult to hold your hand before going across the street," instead of "Don't cross the street alone."

- **Set the timer.** To thrive in today's world, children must have a sense of time, but awareness of time is a programmed skill that is most easily learned after six years of age. Use a single-ring timer to help your child develop a sense of time. Set the timer for five minutes if you want you child to start or stop a behavior in that amount of time, for example.

Uncle Dan's Report Card was the only thing that stopped my child from biting and pushing in preschool. Using it calmed her down.

—MOTHER OF A THREE-YEAR-OLD, UNCLE DAN'S
REPORT CARD KANSAS PILOT PROGRAM

Takeaways!

- No positive consequences result from spanking. In fact, the link between the victimization of children and subsequent anger-management problems underscores the argument for creating a zero-tolerance policy in your home, at day care, in preschool, and in other settings. However, creating a zero-tolerance policy should not result in a criminal penalty for spanking. Instead, this policy should be a statement of your own beliefs that discipline should be a teaching system that builds appropriate behavior.

- Child development experts report that children who live with firm, fairly enforced rules are more secure than children with unlimited freedom. A lack of rules is frightening because, without guidelines, children don't know what to expect.

- Stanley Milgram's research found that if an authority figure tells you to inflict pain on another person, that authority can overcome your deeply held moral beliefs against hurting other people. Children see the world in concrete terms. When they see it's permissible for adults to hit children, they assume it must be permissible for children to hit adults or other children.

- Being on time is a crucial factor in creating a good first impression, whether on a job interview, getting to class in school, or meeting others for the first time. Promptness is the universally accepted axiom of the "golden rule" (do to others what you would like them to do to you!) of manners in action. It is respectful to others not to make them wait—time is precious, so waiting is wasting a most valuable resource.

Habits of Kindness

Kindness is the basis of all the social virtues—politeness, gentleness, etc., and also of cheerfulness, unselfishness, trustworthiness, sense of responsibility, honor, chivalry, democracy, and self-sacrifice.

—*THE MOTHERS' BOOK: SUGGESTIONS REGARDING
THE MENTAL AND MORAL DEVELOPMENT OF CHILDREN,*
BY CAROLINE BENEDICT BURRELL, 1909

Why "Habits of Kindness" Mattered Then

We think that C. T. Grawn, president of the Central Normal School in Michigan, in 1909, would have loved that "Habits of Kindness" was on Uncle Dan's Home Report. He noted, "It has doubtless come within the observation of every teacher that the American youth is not at all times as courteous and as kind as he ought to be. No better recommendation can be taken out into life by a young man or woman than the fact that they are courteous and kind in all their relations with their fellow beings. The school and the home should help the child in the formation of these vital habits."

Uncle Dan certainly learned the habit well. He told us on his ninetieth birthday that the secret to staying healthy throughout your life is to be helpful to your clients and friends, and treat people like you wanted to be treated yourself.

Perhaps he started learning this habit when he was only three years old, as Caroline Burrell of *The Mothers' Book* notes: "Until a child is nearly three years, she seldom has imagination enough to begin to be really kind. You may teach him not to pull the cat's tail; but that's because he is obedient, or because he's afraid of being scratched. When he is nearly three, he can begin to imagine how it would feel to be pussy and have his tail pulled. This is the beginning of kindness."

Why "Habits of Kindness" Matters Today

We exist in a highly competitive world in which winning at all costs is the norm. Popular television today features many shows dedicated to competition as contestants try to destroy each other to win the prize. Lying, cheating, and stealing are the norm, rather than the exception.

Many children expect to be given everything, without doing anything on their part to help others. Encouraging children to be helpful and to do more that simply think about what they want to do will teach them to be aware of the needs of others and give them practice in the fine art of having empathy.

Kindness reinforces our feeling of belonging to a group

and results in an uplifting sensation that feels so good that we want to do it over and over again. It is how the population sustains itself in good times and in bad. Something happens inside us when we commit an act of kindness that results in good heath. As in the famous story of Dorothy, who was seeking the path back "home" in her search for the "wonderful Wizard of Oz," the way to achieve a sense of well-being truly lies within us. Nobody's born with prejudice and unkindness built in. It's in the best interest of us all to practice habits of kindness.

The key to kindness is empathy, an ability to imagine what another person is feeling. Empathy is required to live by the "Golden Rule," which says we should treat others as we would like to be treated. But is it possible to be immersed in the hardwired culture of today and continue to have empathy? Staying electronically connected is like living in a cocoon with little actual human connection. Communicating only by text, tweet, and email lacks the emotional connection that face-to-face contact has, as discussed in Habit 12, "Manners," on page 97. How can you feel empathy for the other person if you can't see her face, hear her voice, read her body language?

Electronic communication also allows people to be relatively anonymous because they don't have to face the other person when they are being unkind, and lack awareness of how their rude or thoughtless comments or behavior are actually hurting another person. The belief that one is anonymous can also be dangerous when people decide not to follow traffic rules or send emails that they think no one else will read except the intended receiver. As we devote less and less time for our imagination to run free in our "task-oriented world," could empathy be in danger of becoming extinct? All people are born with the ability to have empathy, but that ability must be nurtured in order to develop habits of kindness.

HOW TO TEACH A CHILD HABITS OF KINDNESS TODAY

- **Be an Uncle Dan.** Children learn by watching the adults in their world, so it is imperative to develop your own habits of kindness. Your model and that of teachers, baby-sitters, grandparents, and child care providers are the most important influences in training your children how to behave kindly each day. Treat children with respect by listening to them, showing empathy, and understanding their point of view, each of which encourages them to repeat these behaviors.

- **Establish family kindness goals.** Talk about and plan acts of kindness your family can do together, such as donating cans of food, picking up weeds in a neighbor's yard, or visiting a friend whose pet is sick to cheer her up. Not only will your child learn kindness from your example, but he will also practice his natural empathy.

- **Praise, praise, praise.** When you see your child behaving kindly, point out the behavior and tell your child how much you appreciate his kindness.

✏ **Point out kindness in others.** If you see others in your community acting kindly, point out the kindness and say how kindness affects others. Say, for example, "It was so kind of our neighbor to bring fresh tomatoes from his garden. His kindness makes me feel so good."

✏ **Practice makes habit.** If your child behaves unkindly, point out the inappropriate behavior, and ask your child to practice doing the kind thing. For example, if he pulls the dog's tail, show him how to be kind to the dog by petting him nicely together.

✏ **Ask for your child's help.** Say, "I need your help to take out the trash," for example. Telling your child that you need her help lets her know that she is an important contributing member of the family and encourages empathy.

If I want my children to grow up knowing how to do these things, I need to start teaching them now.

—PARENT OF TODDLERS, UNCLE DAN'S REPORT
CARD KANSAS PILOT PROGRAM

📖 Takeaways!

- Empathy is key to developing emotional intelligence, as described by Daniel Goleman in his books *Emotional Intelligence* and *Social Intelligence*.

- Tell your child, "I love you" every day, and treat her with kindness without your child "doing" any particular thing at all! We all need to know that we are loved by our mother and father, as well as other caring adults in our lives. Telling a child, "I love you," is a priceless gift of kindness she'll never forget and will always keep inside her as a source of comfort in good times and in bad.

- Research in child development has found that mothers' use of anger to control their children chips away at the child's ability to feel empathy.

- Kindness is contagious. When one person treats another with respect, both win: the giver and the receiver are reinforced to repeat the behavior.

- Reinforce your child's ability to care about others' feelings by pointing out how they might feel in a situation, why they might think differently from another person, and how "understanding" doesn't always mean "agreeing" with another's point of view. You can agree to disagree.

Truthfulness and Honesty

The common school is the place of all others to inculcate the great industrial, social and civic virtues of honesty, chastity, truthfulness, justice, responsibility for social order, all the moral safeguard of national life.

—ETHEL ANDERSON, PRINCIPAL, ARMSTRONG SCHOOL,
KANSAS CITY, KANSAS, SCHOOL DISTRICT, 1911

Why "Truthfulness and Honesty" Mattered Then

On the subject of Truthfulness and Honesty, Tillie gave Dan E's for "Excellent" throughout the period. If *The Mothers' Book* was her guide, she would have read:

Honesty, also, must be strenuously insisted upon. Let the children understand thoroughly that it is stealing to take the smallest thing belonging to another. The principle must be rigidly maintained in the family. The surprising carelessness of some parents in allowing their children to appropriate anything at home which they may desire lays the foundation of dishonesty, or, at least, of indifference to the rights of others. It is strange, but nevertheless a fact, that children of the most irreproachable parents, unless early taught to despise lying and stealing, will lack both truth and honesty in the same proportion as the offspring of unprincipled parents.

The educators who created Uncle Dan's report card understood that "Right Concepts," such as honesty, must be taught by home and school. It was clear that they understood the concept of teachable moments. To encourage the development of honest behavior, M. E. Pearson assigned a committee to help him prepare a "Course of Study in Social Ethics for the Grade Schools and High Schools." The course was arranged by grades in monthly periods of four topics each, and was published in a 61-page pamphlet. The course outlined several "aims" and provided practical suggestions for teaching them. For example, the goal of Aim No. 3:

To Develop Right Concepts: Pupils usually know right from wrong, but they need to have their concepts clarified and extended. If they have been wisely taught at home and at school, they react habitually in the right ways without knowing the reason for their conduct. As they enter the reasoning period of youth, they need to have their conduct rationalized.

Practical Suggestion No. 2:

Every subject taught furnishes opportunities for teaching ethics and unless these opportunities are utilized to apply ideals, the direct teaching will be handicapped. In arithmetic, teach thrift, accuracy, and truth . . . in nature study, teach truth, beauty, and reverence, etc. Put life, vigor, vim, humor, truth, love, and beauty into these lessons. "Tempt pupils to righteousness."

Dan learned these lessons well. He graduated from Michigan Law School with the highest of honors, and had a successful career as an attorney and a judge. When interviewed by local reporters on his ninetieth birthday, he was asked to define success. "Success is being recognized as a person with whom people like to do business," he answered.

He loved telling the story of how he was appointed judge when the judge holding the elected office died. When it was time for Dan to run for reelection, the head of Kansas City's corrupt political machine called Dan to his office. "We will help you win the election if you do things our way," Dan remembers him saying.

"No thank you," Dan responded, knowing that he would probably be asked to behave dishonestly. "And I lost the election," he would say with a prideful smile.

Why "Truthfulness and Honesty" Matters Today

If honesty is the best policy, how can a child reconcile being surrounded by the dishonest behavior of adults in programs they watch on television reality shows, newscasts, tweets, blogs, and advertising? They see commercials encouraging parents to be dishonest with their children so they don't know they are actually eating vegetables or whole grains in their favorite foods. Cheating is rampant and described by high school and college students as necessary to be able to compete in today's world. Truthfulness and honesty have been sacrificed at the altar of success, of winning at all costs.

In the connected world of email, tweets, and texts, it has become much easier to lie because of the lack of face-to-face contact in communication. It is more difficult to lie when looking in another person's eyes. People begin to believe they can stay anonymous when violating traffic laws, conducting business online, and lying on social media sites.

Deterioration of a neighborhood has often been attributed to "the broken window" effect. In short, broken windows in buildings and houses give tacit permission to break more windows, litter, and vandalize, because it is obvious nobody cares. The same effect may be at work when we see people in leadership positions lie, cheat, and steal. Such behavior simply gives permission for others to do the same. People in high positions of power may ultimately believe that they are above the law and need answer to no one.

Adolescents are less influenced by the behavior of people in power than they are by their peers. Acceptance by peers is paramount in the adolescent world, perhaps because humans are hardwired to live in groups, so being rejected by peers is seen as being thrown to the wolves. As a result, adolescents will be more likely to follow group norms than rules set by adults. Adolescents also have a limited view of the future, so following rules today so they can be successful in the future becomes difficult.

HOW TO TEACH A CHILD TRUTHFULNESS AND HONESTY

- **Be an Uncle Dan.** Even when you are tempted to take the easy way out and stretch the truth, remind yourself that your children need you to be a good example: Obey traffic laws; avoid saying you're out of Popsicles just because you don't want to say no to your child's request; and above all, be truthful when talking to others.

- **Praise, praise, praise.** When your child tells the truth, praise his behavior. The best praise is simply describing the behavior and telling your child you appreciate what she or he has done, instead of praising the child himself: "Thanks for telling the truth when we asked who tracked mud into the house."

- **Point out honesty you see in others.** Life is full of examples of truthfulness and honesty. When you see an example, describe what you saw and say how important it was. For example say, "When I asked your friend if she had spilled her drink in your room, she said she had and that she was very sorry. That was so nice that she was truthful."

- **Avoid forcing the lie by asking a question that you already know the answer to.** When you ask your child if he has any homework and you already know that he does, you've forced him to weigh the question and take a chance that you will believe him if he says no. You may be encouraging lying by asking a question when you already know the answer. Such questions are traps to encourage confession, which has not been found to be at all helpful in building honesty. Instead, ask a specific question about homework that will encourage a positive result, for example: "Can I help you practice your spelling words?" or "Can I see your homework assignments?"

- **Show the harm of dishonesty.** Look for examples on TV and in your daily life of the harmful effects of dishonesty. Discuss examples of cheating, lying, and the dishonest manipulation often seen on TV and the consequences of those actions. Talk about the lies often told about people on social media sites and the damage those lies can do.

The Report Card finally gives parents and teachers something to work with in concert. Use this to inculcate these behaviors in our children.

—PRINCIPAL OF AN ELEMENTARY SCHOOL, UNCLE
DAN'S REPORT CARD KANSAS PILOT PROGRAM

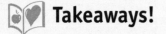 **Takeaways!**

- Model truthfulness and honesty, and tell your child why you have been tempted to tell a lie. Say, "I returned the money to the cashier who gave me too much change, even though I would have liked to have kept it. I wanted to be honest. It feels good to tell the truth."

- Explain how truthfulness and honesty build trust between people. Give instances from your own life—for example, when someone lied to you and how you can't trust what he says anymore.

- When your child doesn't tell the truth, talk calmly with her about the situation. Ask what she learned from the situation, how she felt about telling a lie, and how she could tell the truth if she was in this situation again. Role-playing honesty is a good way to focus on what you want your child to learn, not what mistakes he made.

Acknowledgments

Gratitude is a quality similar to electricity: it must be produced and discharged and used up in order to exist at all.

—WILLIAM FAULKNER

Our good friend, Jerry Wyckoff, PhD, has been our trusted and generous partner in our parenting books and projects for over three decades. We thank him for his caring and concern for children's health and well-being, which was so profoundly valuable during our Uncle Dan's Report Card pilot program and the writing of this book.

Kindly keeping our enthusiasm focused and his mind open to all possibilities, Perigee's publisher, John Duff, has been an honest, soulful, and dedicated champion of bringing this 1914 treasure to life within this book and beyond. Thanks, John, for your steadfast steering of the ship . . . and your cheerful companionship in the world of publishing for so many years. Jeanette Shaw and Joan Matthews found the balance we needed as our thoughtful editor and copyeditor, making sure we kept our material relevant and rooted in the practical for today's generations. As Uncle Dan would say, "Wowzee!"

How fortunate we have been to benefit from the wise counsel of many dedicated teachers, child advocates, administrators, and researchers, including: Jonathan Haidt and Sara Rimm-Kaufman of the University of Virginia; Jesse Graham of the University of Southern California; Michael Weiler of the Shawnee Mission School District; Mark Weiss and Peter Yarrow of Operation Respect; Millie Wyckoff, former kindergarten teacher; Tom Trigg, superintendent of the Blue Valley School District; Jay Winsten of the Harvard School of Public Health and the Center for Health Communications; Patricia Adams of Kansas City, Kansas, Public Schools; Monte Gross of the Wyandotte County Museum; Wendy Webb of Kansas Parents As Teachers; Mary Lou Anderson, early childhood educator; Ellen Hamilton Zuniga, former Montessori school principal; and Jane Warren, former elementary school teacher.

We would also like to express our appreciation to the helpful staffs of the Kenneth Spencer Research Library and the Watson Library at the University of Kansas; the Kansas City, Kansas, Library; and the Kansas Historical Society.

Special gratitude goes to the Kansas PTA's Peggy Davis, Lauri Denooy, and Laura Kaiser.

The following civic leaders have provided their unwavering friendship and support: former governor of Kansas Kathleen Sebelius; former U.S. Congressman Dennis Moore and Stephene Moore; Cynthia Wendt of Congressman Moore's office; U.S. Congressman Emanuel Cleaver; former Kansas State Senator Audrey Langworthy;

Johnson County, Kansas, Commissioner David Lindstrom; Former Kansas State Senator Richard Bond; the Dockhorn Family; Harold and Marilyn Melcher; Alan Edelman; Karen Gerson; Laura McKnight, CEO and President, Greater Kansas City Community Foundation; Spence Heddens; and former news anchor Lili Shank.

Deep appreciation goes to our Uncle Dans—Mary Shaw "Shawsie" Branton, Adele Hall, Bob and Ann Regnier, Fred and Shirley Pryor, and Walt and Jackie Eggers.

Thanks to those who helped us with their talent and imagination as we explored the infinite ways we could bring Uncle Dan's Report Card to the twenty-first century, including: Frank Addington; Renee Andriani; Bethany Doulis; Neal Sharma and Terese Babcock of Digital Evolution Group; Eddie Hall; David Moore; Marcie Setlow; Howard, Jennifer, and Barclay Martin; the team at Hallmark Cards Inc. led by Teddi Hernandez; and Gaye Bredemeier and Brian Loube of Our365.

A special tribute to those who first planted the seeds for this book, when we were youngsters ourselves, including our grandparents, parents, extended family, childhood mentors and teachers, youth leaders, and coaches.

Finally, our heartfelt gratitude to the too numerous to name, but all so dear, family members and friends of Uncle Dan, in particular Larry and Holly Brenner, and Marvin and Marilyn Brenner.

And as always, we are inspired by our beloved children, Amy Elizabeth Unell and Justin Alex Unell. We delight in their taking the lessons of Uncle Dan to heart and carrying on his legacy.

Index

Index

books (*cont.*)
  importance of, 32
  list of, 33
  reading, 31–35
  teaching children about, 33–34
  in Uncle Dan's library, 31
Brenner, Daniel Leon, xiv, 12
Brenner, Harry, 12
Brenner, Tillie, xiii, 14
bribing habits, 29
Brokaw, Tom, 7
broken window effect, 146
budgets, 54
Burrell, Caroline Benedict, 31, 97, 130, 137, 143–44

Care and Feeding of Children (Holt), 13, 92
Cathcart, Margaret, 130
Central Normal School, 137
Century of the Child, The (Key), 12
  home occupations in, 118
  modern mothers in, 119
  sharing work in, 105
charity, 61
cheating habits, 146–47
checklists, 78
Child Life, Physical and Mental Development, 123–24
child psychology, 13
child-rearing habits
  in *Anxious Parents*, 76, 81
  science of, 11–15
children
  academic performance of, 74
  accidents of, 70
  allowance for, 53
  American, twentieth-century, 61
  anger-management problems in, 135
  attention spans of, 32
  bathing attitudes of, 82
  bedtime routines of, 94–95
  books for, 31

  bribing of, 29
Care and Feeding of Children, 13, 92
  communication with, 27
  contribution of, household, 46–47
  crafts made by, 63–67
  developing character of, ix
  earning money, 51
  encouraging money saving habits in, 58–59
  environment of, 8
  evening hours with, 69
  Federal Children's Bureau, 13
  feelings of, 28
  healthy, 6
  home life of, 3
  imagination of, 67
  letter writing for, 41–42
  manners of, 97–102
  nagging of, 30
  needs of, 19–20
  obedience in, 129–34
  overindulged, 55
  parental honesty with, 147
  parents bathing, 84
  parents hitting, 135
  promptness in, 129–34
  punishment of, 29–30
  reinforcing habits of, x
  rules for, 6, 135
  schedules of, 72
  shaming of, 29
  sickness in, 92
  teaching books to, 33–34
  teaching budget to, 54
  teaching clothing care to, 87–89
  teaching credit cards to, 58–59
  teaching good behavior to, 4–5
  teaching honesty to, 147–49
  teaching material possessions to, 55
  teaching money to, 53–54
  teaching morning duties to, 120–21
  teaching teeth care to, 77
  teaching time to, 134–35

Index

Index

Index

University of California Los Angeles
  American consumption research
    from, 61
  lessons/sports research by, 74
University of Michigan research
  program, 35
University of Missouri Board of
  Curators, xii
University of Virginia, 103

values, moral
  American, 11
  American, immigrants' adoption
    of, 18–20
  books with, 31
  of children, x
  guidelines of, 9
  importance of, 10
  in *The Mothers' Book*, 31
  for work, 48–49
verbal responses, 132–33
Virginia Department of Psychology,
  4–5

Wallace, Emma Gary, 57
Wilder, Thornton, xi

windows
  open, during sleep, 91–96
  screens for, 93
work
  for allowance, 53
  attitudes about, 50
  baby-sitting, 52
  in *The Century of the Child*, 105
  ethic, Uncle Dan's, 105
  homework, 124–25
  hours of, 45–50
  importance of, 45–46
  mentors for, 50
  moral values for, 48–49
  motivation for, 47–48, 50
  outside home, 51
  over pleasure, 28
  parent schedules for, 107
  in *Pricing the Priceless Child*, 45,
    117
  teaching value of, 48–49
Wright Edelman, Marion, 21

Yale University, 132

Zelizer, Viviana, 45, 51, 70, 117

About the Authors

BARBARA C. UNELL

Barbara C. Unell has spent the past thirty years as a mother, editor, author, and educator passionately motivating adults to model and teach children kindness, respect, and compassion. She has been the coauthor of over a dozen parenting books—each fostering positive family relationships as well as social and emotional well-being— ranging from the 1974 guidebook *Competency-Based Teacher Edu-*

cation to *Discipline Without Shouting or Spanking* (1984, 2002), to *20 Teachable Virtues* (1995) and 2004's *Getting Your Child from No to Yes Without Nagging, Bribing, or Threatening.*

Barbara is also one of the creators of the nationally acclaimed character education program "Kindness Is Contagious . . . Catch It!" which has taught kindness, respect, and compassion to thousands of children throughout the Kansas City area and across the country since its inception in 1990.

Founder of Sunflower Celebration, a program of the Blue Valley Educational Foundation in Overland Park, Kansas, Barbara has worked with families in the Blue Valley School District in Overland Park for more than twenty years to honor students and staff for their demonstration of the seven Blue Valley Virtues.

In 1997, Barbara opened the Daniel L. Brenner Family Education Center. The center was named in honor of the distinguished judge and lawyer Daniel L. Brenner, her uncle and own role model of devotion to family and character education. Partnering with Kansas Governor Kathleen Sebelius and U.S. Congressman Dennis Moore, Barbara and Bob Unell piloted Uncle Dan's Report Card in 2005, a program that guides and supports parents in modeling and teaching children personal responsibility, learning readiness, and social skills.

Along with Bob, Barbara served as an adjunct professor at the Communications Studies Department at the University of Missouri-Kansas City from 2001 to 2003. She has also appeared on hundreds of local media and on national television, in print, and on radio, including *The Oprah Winfrey Show*, *NBC Nightly News*, *Good Morning America*, *Today*, *CBS Evening News*, *CBS Early Show*, NPR, the Associated Press Radio Network, *USA Today*, *Time*, *Good Housekeeping*, *Parents*, *Newsweek*, and the *New York Times*.

BOB UNELL

After teaching art in the Kansas City Public Schools, Bob began his twenty-five-year career in the marketing communications field working for three Kansas City advertising agencies. In 1984, he founded his own firm, Unell Associates. That same year, Bob, with his wife, Barbara, parents of twins, cofounded the national magazine for parents of multiples, *Twins*. In 1986, the couple launched *Kansas City Parent Magazine*.

In 2000, Bob and Barbara established Back in the Swing, the first and only national nonprofit organization providing grassroots awareness, education, and fund-raising on behalf of the more than two and a half million breast cancer survivors in the United States.

Along with Barbara, Bob served as an adjunct professor at the Communications Studies Department at the University of Missouri-Kansas City from 2001 to 2003.

In March 2001, Bob fulfilled a childhood dream of being a cartoonist, by launching a weekly editorial cartoon in the Kansas City Star's STAR Business Weekly. His cartoons have appeared annually in the annual Best Editorial Cartoons of the Year since 2004.

About the Authors

He joined Barbara in 2005 to launch the Uncle Dan's Report Card pilot program in three Kansas school districts. Bob has performed the role of "Uncle Dan," sharing the healthy habits on Uncle Dan's Report Card with elementary school students throughout the Kansas City area.

For more information, go to UncleDansReportCard.org.